Livebearers

Livebearers

Understanding Guppies, Mollies,
Swordtails, and Others

David Alderton

BOWTIE™
P R E S S

Irvine, California

Published in 2004 by BowTie Press
A Division of BowTie, Inc.
3 Burroughs, Irvine, CA 92618
www.bowtiepress.com
Fish Keeping Made Easy is an imprint of BowTie Press

Produced by Andromeda Oxford Limited
Kimber House
1 Kimber Road
Abingdon
Oxon OX14 1SG.
www.andromeda.co.uk

Project Director: Graham Bateman. Managing Editor: Shaun Barrington.
Editing and design: D & N DTP and Editorial Services.
Cartography: Tim Williams. Indexer: Sheila Seacroft
Picture Manager: Claire Turner. Production: Clive Sparling.

Library of Congress Cataloging-in-Publication Data
Alderton, David, 1956-
    Livebearers / by David Alderton.
        p. cm. -- (Fishkeeping made easy)
Includes bibliographical references (p.   ) and index.
    ISBN 1-931993-19-X (hardcover : alk. paper)
    1. Livebearing aquarium fishes. I. Title. II. Series.
    SF458.L58A58 2003
    639.3'7667--dc21
                                            2003013120

Page 2: Merry widow (*Phallichthys amates amates*).
Cover: Tuxedo multi-color snakeskin guppy, (*Poecilia reticulata* var.); Max Gibbs/Photomax.

Photographic credits

Andromeda Oxford Limited 71 x4, 85; Dennis Barrett 35, 40, 42; John Dawes 22; © www.Hippocampus-Bildarchiv.de 2, 9b, 10–11, 12–13, 13, 14, 16, 17, 18–19, 23, 24–25, 26, 27, 28t, 28b, 29, 30t, 30b, 31, 32, 33, 34, 36t, 36b, 37, 41, 43, 44, 45, 46, 47, 50, 51t, 51b, 52, 53, 54–55, 55t, 55b, 57, 75, 82, 87, 96, 107, 109, 110, 120, 121, 124, 125, 127, 128, 129, 130, 131, 132, 133, 134, 135, 137; D. Lambert 122; Aldo Brando/Oxford Scientific Films 9c; Peter Gathercole/Oxford Scientific Films 99; Max Gibbs/Photomax 3, 7, 15, 21, 38, 39, 48, 49, 56, 60–61, 66–67, 68, 73, 74–75t, 74–75b, 77, 78, 81, 83, 92, 100, 103, 117, 119, 123, 126, 136; Mike Sandford 88, 91, 112, 115, 118; Jane Burton/Warren Photographic 84, 90, 98, 104, 106, 114.

Color origination by Grasmere Digital Imaging Ltd., Leeds.
Printed in Hong Kong by Paramount Printing Ltd.

Contents

Nature and Nurture 6

1 Where in the World? 8
An ancient tradition 8
Patterns of distribution 9
Breeding potential 10
From the sea to freshwater 11
Lifestyles of livebearers 12
Predation and adaptation 14
Parasites and pairing 16
Foreign introductions of livebearers 17
Endangered species 18

2 The Different Groups 20
Making Choices 21
Be patient! 25
Classification 25
Family Goodeidae: goodeids or
    Mexican livebearers 29
Family Anablepidae: four-eyes and
    related species 37
Family Poeciliidae: guppies and
    related species 39
Family Hemirhamphidae: halfbeaks 55

3 Characteristics and Care 58
Defining characteristics 58
Other sensory organs 59
Respiration 61
Fin structures 61
The copulatory organ 62
Housing options 65
Positioning the aquarium 66
Plan ahead 67
How many fish? 68
Filtration systems 68
Heating control 70
Lighting 72
Aquarium gravel 72
Planting schemes 74
Choosing aquarium plants 74
Planting considerations 76
Rocks and woodwork 77
Water chemistry 79
Other special housing needs 83

4 Feeding Habits and Food 84
Mouthparts 84
The digestive tract and diet 85
Greenstuff 86
Color foods 86
Live foods 87
Meat 91
Varying the diet 91

5 Reproduction 92
Breeding success 92
Reproductive habits 93
Size and survival 95
Hybridization 95
Mate choice 98
Gender determination 99
Other reproductive triggers 101
Brood size 101
The breeding environment 102
Rearing the young 105
Growth rates 106
Genetics 107

6 Lifespan and Diseases 110
Lifespan and temperature 110
Signs of aging 110
Treatment tanks 111
Signs of illness 112
Fungal diseases 112
Bacterial diseases 113
Parasites 115
Noninfectious illness 118

7 Popular Livebearers 120
Family Goodeidae 120
Family Anablepidae 123
Family Poeciliidae 124
Family Hemirhamphidae 137

Further Reading 138
Websites 138
Glossary 139
Index 141

Nature and Nurture

The group of fish known as livebearers features some of the most attractive and fascinating species now gracing aquariums throughout the world. Their popularity today would have no doubt surprised and delighted those who are credited with discovering them in the wild and bringing them to the attention of zoologists.

IN THE BEGINNING

Tropical fishkeeping as a hobby did not really start in earnest until the early 20th century, and in the beginning it was a perilous pursuit. Tanks were designed with slate bases and heated by gas, relying on a naked flame for this purpose. This meant that accurate temperature control of the water was impossible, and dramatic and sometimes fatal fluctuations occurred. Livebearers as a group are, however, much better suited than many fish to adapting to this type of variable environment because it is not dissimilar to the conditions under which a number of species live in the wild. Livebearers often inhabit shallow stretches of water, which can be heated up rapidly by the sun, so they may be subjected to marked variations in water temperature. They are also quite adaptable in terms of their water chemistry needs.

It was as a result of their tolerance that livebearers soon became popular. Yet there was also another, more fundamental reason, why they became prominent during the early days of the aquarium hobby and have retained their preeminent position. At the outset, there were none of the special diets that are available to fish keepers today, and this meant that rearing the young of egg-laying fish could be especially problematic. In the case of the commonly kept livebearers, however, they needed relatively little care. While eggs could be afflicted by fungus, there was no risk of this problem with livebearers. And as they are relatively large at birth the fry themselves were quite easy to rear. They matured rapidly and would in turn breed repeatedly, without requiring the conditioning triggers that prove necessary in the case of egg-layers.

FAMOUS FIND

The Reverend John Guppy recorded the wild form of what has since become the best known of all livebearers, and now bears his name, on the Caribbean island of Trinidad just off the northern coast of South America around 1865. He subsequently brought live specimens back to Britain. Ironically, however, in this particular case these fish had previously been recorded two years earlier, by a Spaniard called De Filippi, whose discovery of them is now largely forgotten.

DEVELOPMENT OF THE HOBBY

It was not until after the end of World War II in 1945 that tropical fishkeeping entered a new era. Florida became the main center for breeding such fish on a commercial scale, thanks partly to its climate and also its geographical position—close to Central and South America, where desirable fish, including livebearers, could be obtained. The market expanded as ex-combat pilots returned home and began to fly regular shipments from Florida's growing number of tropical fish farms to other states in the U.S. and up to Canada.

Aquarium-keeping started to develop on an unprecedented scale as a result, and the popular livebearers—such as guppies, swordtails, mollies, and platies—were ideal to meet this demand. Breeders started to create more colorful fish, and this led to the establishment of shows; these still take place regularly in Florida, and allow breeders to display the newest variants. It is not just the color of the fish that has been modified—fin shapes and body types have been altered too. In a number of cases, the close relationships between the different species of livebearers has led to hybridization as well, which has accelerated the process of creating new forms of these fish, far brighter and more varied in appearance than their ancestors.

Today's domesticated bloodlines of the most popular species are far removed from the wild forms, and yet livebearers as a group also offer considerable appeal to the specialist breeder who is interested in keeping and studying fish about which little is known. This applies particularly in the case of the halfbeaks, which belong to the family Hemirhamphidae. So whether you are just starting out with an aquarium or are a longstanding enthusiast, livebearers will be of interest, particularly as a number of species can also be included in a community aquarium alongside other fish.

➊ Tropical fish keeping brings the beauty of the natural world into millions of homes worldwide. Throughout this book, insights into natural fish behavior are emphasized. Understanding how a fish lives in the wild leads to a better understanding of how it should be looked after in captivity. In this case, nurture follows nature.

CHAPTER 1

Where in the World?

Trying to classify fish on the basis of their breeding behavior actually creates inevitable inconsistencies. The use of the term "livebearer" has, in many ways, simply become a convenient shorthand description for a group of four families of aquarium fish. Essentially, therefore, the definition of "livebearer" relates more specifically to aquarium fish, rather than to the world of fish in general.

AN ANCIENT TRADITION

In total, 14 families of fish reproduce by bearing live young. This is actually a characteristic more closely linked with primitive fish, such as the ancient coelacanth (*Latimeria chalumnae*). This particular marine species was believed to have been extinct for nearly 60 million years, when a living example was discovered off the southeastern coast of Africa in 1938. It is striking that over 50 percent of all cartilaginous fish, a grouping that includes sharks and rays, reproduce by means of live young, whereas less than 3 percent of the more recently evolved bony fish retain this method of reproduction.

The reason why most members of the livebearer category give birth to live young may be linked back to their origins. While it is, unfortunately, difficult to piece together a clear picture of how they evolved, there is little disagreement that the group as a whole developed from marine ancestors. This is reflected not just by the fact that some of these fish are found in brackish and saltwater environments today, but rather by assessing the group as a whole. Overwhelmingly—albeit with certain exceptions such as the half-beaks (Hemirhamphidae)—even those that live in freshwater prefer relatively hard, alkaline surroundings, more akin to seawater, than soft, acidic waters.

Further evidence to support the view that the ancestors of today's livebearing families originally inhabited the sea can be derived from the fact that nearly a third of all Poeciliinae species can successfully

🠹 The coelacanth (*Latimeria chalumnae*) is a living fossil, which gives birth to live young.

be acclimatized to live in the marine environment, although barely 3 percent of them are normally found in this habitat. A slightly higher percentage occupy brackish water, where they live naturally under less saline conditions than their marine relatives.

Contemporary livebearers have two areas of natural distribution. The greatest number of species is to be found in the Americas, ranging from the U.S. and Central America into southern parts of South America. The halfbeaks, forming the family Hemirhamphidae, occur in Southeast Asia and represent an older, separate lineage.

PATTERNS OF DISTRIBUTION

The major influence that shaped the distribution of the livebearer group today occurred as a result of the changes that took place in the vicinity of modern day Central America. The original link between the North and South American continents was broken about 30 million years ago. Evidence of this first land bridge is manifested today by various Caribbean islands, notably Cuba and Hispaniola. Some of the livebearers found here today, including Cuban endemics such as *Girardinus* spp. (which occur nowhere else), may represent some of the oldest surviving livebearer lineages in the region.

Being relatively small fish, it is perhaps not surprising that the ancestors of today's livebearers in the area colonized the shallow but tidal mangrove swamps, doubtless hiding away in the roots of the vegetation here. Living so close to the shore, some of these fish would then have started to move inland, from estuaries up streams and rivers, where they ultimately encountered freshwater. There is DNA evidence from Trinidad that guppy populations on the island did not originate from a single period of colonization but that several waves of invasion took place, separated by periods of anything from 100,000 to 600,000 years.

The ancestral livebearers also extended down the coast of northern South America, encountering similar conditions and establishing themselves in this region too. Indeed, not all members of the group have changed their lifestyle significantly, as in the case of the Anablepidae family. While *Anableps microlepis* still lives in the sea here, ranging from the Orinoco to the Amazon rivers, the related species *A. anableps* has crossed into the adjacent brackish area, with its distribution now extending into freshwater too.

◑ Rivers like the Orinoco in northern South America allowed the original marine livebearers to move into freshwater habitats. The Orinoco is just one of the homes of the widespread guppy (*Poecilia reticulata*).

◐ The four-eyed fish (*Anableps anableps*) occurs in brackish areas of water.

More dramatic land changes then probably carried the adaptable livebearers farther inland. This helps to explain why members of today's Goodeidae family, for example, are found in the highlands of Mexico, as the link between the North and South American continents subsequently reformed, around 3 million years ago.

Some of today's most popular livebearers have more recent origins. It is thought that the ancestors of modern day platies and swordtails first developed around a million years ago. The process of speciation, by which populations develop distinctive character-istics and become sufficiently diverse to become recognized as individual species, would then have speeded up as the fish became confined in relatively shallow, small bodies of water. Physical boundaries such as waterfalls also served to isolate the species (and continue to do so), while the drying up of stretches of water may also have played its part during recent geological time in creating the diversity of forms that now exist, as well as con-tributing to the extinction of an unknown number of others.

BREEDING POTENTIAL

The key to the spread of livebearers and development of some of the isolated populations seen today is their reproductive biology. It is not so much the obvious fact that females produce live young that is significant, but rather that they remain fertile potentially for the rest of their lives after a single mating. Consider a situation when just one fertile female fish is swept away during a period of heavy rain and carried, thanks to her small size, into a new stream. Here, once conditions become more settled, she gives birth, estab-lishing a new population in the new environment.

Livebearing therefore represents a very major survival advantage for a species in this situation, compared with reproduction through egg-laying, where both male and female fish must be together on each occasion that mating occurs. There is clear evidence from field studies with endangered poeciliids (*see* page 50) showing that they can colonize new habitats quite successfully as a consequence of their method of reproduction.

FROM THE SEA TO FRESHWATER

While the movement from saltwater to freshwater may not appear to be as dramatic a shift as living at temperatures ranging from near freez-ing up to 81° Fahrenheit (27° Celsius) or so, it does in fact mark a very significant physiological change—salt has a drastic effect on the body.

A fish that lives in the sea faces the problem of preventing too much water from passing out of its body and too much salt entering. This is a result of the process of osmosis, whereby salts pass from a

high concentration to a lower one and water passes from a more dilute to a stronger solution. In addition, marine fish must drink seawater as freshwater is unavailable, and so also accumulate salt in that way. The fish's body responds in various ways to overcome this threat. The gills, for example, actively excrete salt. The kidneys also act to conserve freshwater by producing very little urine. Freshwater is extracted from seawater and drawn into the body from the gut, with the salt passing through unabsorbed, again helping to counter the potentially fatal effects of dehydration in a marine environment.

When a fish is living in freshwater, however, the situation is in effect reversed, with the need to remove water from the body and also conserve salts being paramount. The tissues in this case contain a stronger solution than that in which the fish is swimming, and hence osmosis seeks to draw water into the body rather than out of it. Salts this time are more concentrated inside the fish than they are in the water, and tend to pass out. Fish found in freshwater surroundings therefore produce large quantities of very dilute urine, and their kidneys are adapted to save salts within the body. The gills also actively absorb salts from the water flowing over them.

⬆ Waterfalls present physical barriers to the spread of small fish like livebearers farther upstream from the mouths of estuaries. This is part of the southern habitat of the swordtail (*Xiphophorus helleri*) in Honduras.

LIFESTYLES OF LIVEBEARERS

It is a feature of many livebearers that they have relatively restricted areas of distribution in the wild. They may sometimes occupy small, shallow pools—rather like their killifish relatives—where aquatic invertebrates such as mosquito larvae are numerous, although some

● Guppies (*Poecilia reticulata*) are the most widely kept livebearers today, breeding readily in aquariums. This is a wild variety; for ornate varieties, *see* page 49.

members of the group can equally be encountered in fast-flowing rivers. The adaptable nature of these fish is further reflected by the changes that often occur in their environment through the year. For example, they can face very large differences in the water temperature on a daily basis—as much as 68°F (20°C)—quite apart from longer term seasonal variations. This is because livebearers often live in small bodies of water, which heat up and cool down rapidly. Since they tend to occupy the upper reaches of the water, they are exposed to the widest variations in temperature.

The habitat that livebearers thrive in of course defines their distribution. It is no coincidence that the vast majority of species are small fish. Their size allows them to move into shallow waters, taking advantage of invertebrate foods there, and also means they can live in large groups. As an example, concentrations of huge numbers of mosquito fish (*Gambusia affinis* and *G. holbrooki*) have been documented on various occasions. It has even been reported

UNUSUAL HABITAT

Members of the livebearers' group are found in many different environments, and not just in brackish conditions or freshwater. Certain species, such as *Poecilia sulphuraria*, have even adapted to living in water where the sulfur content is high, as reflected in this case by its scientific name. This species' natural habitat is very limited, being confined to the Arroyo del Azufre, located in the Mexican state of Tabasco. The sulfur in the water here is too strong to support any aquatic vegetation, aside from a particular type of algae that the fish appear to rely on as their main food source. The fish, like the algae, have a distinctly silvery coloration. These unusual environmental conditions have meant that this is one species that has not proved easy to maintain in aquarium surroundings.

that introduced populations in ponds in Italy became so numerous on occasions that cattle were unable to drink there.

Many livebearers inhabit stretches of water where there is little aquatic vegetation present. Such fish will avoid congregating in schools in the upper reaches of the water under these conditions, preferring instead to use whatever natural cover is available to conceal their presence. This means that in the center of the stream they will often stay close to the bottom, hiding among stones and other debris here. They will also seek the protection of overhanging vegetation at the banks. In contrast, however, livebearers that do occur in well-vegetated streams and similar environments are more evenly distributed through their habitat. This behavior has clear implications when setting up an aquarium for these fish. Not only is an attractively planted tank more aesthetically pleasing, but it should also ensure that the fish settle well in these surroundings, rather than lurking in an area where cover is available.

An interesting observation in waters where livebearers have been caught is that within a population there can be a considerable variation in size between individuals, unrelated to their gender. This may well bring survival advantages for the population, since while the smaller fish may be more able to hide away, so their larger companions may be less vulnerable to the pressures of predation. Size is also significant in reproductive terms, since the bigger female livebearers will have correspondingly greater numbers of offspring and can boost the population accordingly. They therefore represent a reserve of genetic power.

Young livebearers face a particular risk of predation, often from their own species as well as others. Consequently, they tend to be encountered in the densest vegetation, often close to the water's edge, where they can slip away undetected. Older fish, on the other hand, are less at risk and so tend to be found throughout the habitat.

As they occur in restricted areas of water, certain livebearers are now regarded as being especially vulnerable to the threats arising from human activity. These can range from water extraction, which affects water levels, to the runoff of fertilizers and pesticides, as well as general industrial pollution, all of which can impact on the aquatic vegetation. But here again, the adaptable biology of livebearers does offer some hope for their survival in the face of adverse environmental conditions—guppies (*Poecilia reticulata*) have even been recorded living in sewage drains.

⊕ Mosquito fish (*Gambusia affinis*) can multiply at an amazing rate under suitable conditions.

PREDATION AND ADAPTATION

As they are relatively close to the bottom of the food chain, populations of livebearers also face pressures of predation as part of the battle for survival. Their relatively small size means that they are vulnerable to a host of possible predators, ranging from turtles and amphibians to birds and even other fish, including *Cichlasoma* spp. of cichlids. While aquarium keepers marvel at the diversity of forms that have been created in livebearers such as guppies (*Poecilia reticulata*), the underlying biological basis for this beauty is simply survival. So-called "plasticity" in guppy populations helps them to resist the assaults of predators such as cichlids, enabling them to adapt to a particular threat in their environment. This phenomenon has been demonstrated through a fascinating series of experiments conducted on wild guppies from different areas of Trinidad.

On this Caribbean island, there are two significant piscine predators of guppies. In stretches of water where the predatory giant rivulus (*Rivulus harti*) predominates, this egg-laying toothcarp—which averages about 4in (10cm) in length—feeds mainly on small young guppies. The guppy populations in such areas tend to be skewed in favor of females, which grow to a significantly larger size than their male counterparts, and there are relatively few young in the population. The guppies occur at quite high densities, since the females themselves are unaffected by predation.

Elsewhere, however, the much larger pike cichlid (*Crenicichla alta*) tends not to hunt young guppies, preferring instead to prey on adult fish. The makeup of guppy populations in stretches of water where pike cichlids abound is therefore quite different. Young fish are common, but the population density is low, with the fish being spread out so that they are harder to hunt. There is also no significant difference between the numbers of male and female guppies.

⊕ The giant rivulus (*Rivulus harti*) is a predatory species, capable of feeding on young guppies but not adults which are too large to fall prey to it.

Further investigations have been carried out to reveal how changes could occur, by altering the impact of the selection pressure imposed by predation. This entailed taking guppies that had originally evolved where pike cichlids were the dominant predator, and placing them in an isolated stretch of water where rivulus were present, but where previously there had been no guppies. The guppies were left here for several years, after which time a number of their descendants were then caught. It emerged that not only had the population of introduced guppies become larger in terms of physical size, but also that the females were producing bigger but fewer offspring in each brood.

Other studies carried out showed that even when kept under identical laboratory conditions, guppies originating from populations that had suffered from rivulus predation still had bigger offspring than those derived from waters populated by pike cichlids. Interestingly, both groups of guppies produced more offspring when they were housed under low stocking densities. They did this not by increasing brood size, but rather by shortening the interval between broods. This has a clear potential significance for aquarium breeding: if the aim is to build up the numbers of a particular line, then the females ought to be kept in spacious surroundings as this should result in them breeding faster.

The researchers recorded greater sociability and fewer aggressive interactions in guppy populations from areas where pike cichlids were the dominant predators, and higher reproductive activity. This indicates that such populations were under greater pressure as the

⬆ Pike cichlids (*Crenicichla alta*) will hunt adult guppies, and have had an intriguing effect on the behavior of these fish in the wild.

○ Ornamental fancy guppies (*Poecilia reticulata*), such as this triangletail variant, are more colorful and also less powerful when swimming, compared with their wild relatives. They would therefore be much more vulnerable to predators in such surroundings.

result of their predation, compared with those that had evolved in the company of rivulus and were relatively safe once they had grown to a large size.

Another line of investigation focused on the coloration of male guppies, and revealed that levels of predation could also influence this aspect of their appearance. Perhaps not surprisingly, the most colorful males were to be found in areas where predation was carried out mainly by rivulus. In contrast, conspicuous coloration was far less apparent in male guppies inhabiting areas where pike cichlids occurred. This conclusion was reinforced by similar research carried out on guppy populations in Venezuela.

Camouflage can also be influenced by predation. Zoologists found that where the gravel substrate was quite coarse, a larger pattern of spots developed over successive generations of guppies, compared with those fish inhabiting areas where the covering on the streambed was much finer. The appearance of the guppies was altering, allowing them to blend in more effectively against their background. This change occurs only in the presence of predators, however, confirming that the appearance of the natural guppy population in the wild is directly shaped by the effects of predation. This was further emphasized when guppies from populations that were heavily predated were moved to nearby waters where they were relatively free from such pressure. Following the move to such an environment, the male fish soon became more colorful.

It has been shown that recognition of their predators is not necessarily an acquired instinct. Certainly in the case of guppies, there is clear evidence to show that this behavior has a genetic basis. This has been proven in laboratory tests involving captive-bred guppies from various wild populations. Those that had naturally suffered heavy predation were more cautious in approaching predators, and were especially careful not to stray too close to the area of the mouth, compared with fish that had not been subjected to such pressure.

PARASITES AND PAIRING

Not all threats to the guppy's survival are the result of predation, however. The microscopic parasite *Gyrodactylus* is spread easily by contact between individuals, and one of the symptoms of this infection is that it causes male guppies to lose color, so they become paler. It has been observed that when selecting a mate, female guppies will select those males that display the brightest coloration. Since *Gyrodactylus* infections are relatively common in the wild and often prove to be fatal, such behavior could have significant implications for the survival of the entire population. By avoiding potentially infectious males, females are safeguarding not just their own health but also that of their offspring. The fact that they make a positive choice in this respect has been demonstrated by laboratory experiments using male fish cured of this ailment, which were still paler in color than previously healthy individuals—these fish were ignored by the females. This in turn probably also helps to explain why male guppies will become more brightly colored under normal conditions where predation is quite light.

FOREIGN INTRODUCTIONS OF LIVEBEARERS

Further evidence for the adaptability of this remarkable group of fish can be found in the way at least 19 different species of livebearer are now established in foreign locations, often far away from their natural habitats and in places where they can also face heavy predation. Many of these populations have been established for over half a century, dating back to the time when it became fashionable to introduce them in order to exert a biological control over mosquito populations.

The western and eastern mosquitofish (*Gambusia affinis* and *G. holbrooki* respectively), which used to be considered as a single species, are now established on every continent apart from Antarctica as a consequence of such policies. These fish were even dropped directly by US military planes into remote freshwater localities on various Pacific islands during World War II. Unfortunately, their value in controlling mosquitoes has proved limited, and they may prey on young fish of native species in preference, with consequent harmful impacts on those popula-

◐ Livebearers such as the eastern mosquito fish (*Gambusia holbrooki*) have been used with variable success as a means of biological control, well outside their natural range.

tions. Guppies (*Poecilia reticulata*) were also tried for the purpose of mosquito control, but proved to be a failure in this regard.

Many other livebearers are now thriving across various continents in tropical regions in particular, thanks to being deliberately released. Such fish can represent a serious threat, not just to unrelated fish but also to native populations of livebearers if they are liberated into the same areas. The fact that livebearers can be restricted to small localities means that they are potentially vulnerable in the face of competition.

ENDANGERED SPECIES

There are approximately 14 naturally occurring poeciliids found in the U.S., of which eight are restricted to the states of Texas, Arizona, and New Mexico. Out of this total, over half are subject to endangered species legislation. Recovery plans have been established in an attempt to safeguard their futures, and the Dexter National Fish Hatchery in southeastern New Mexico is now being used to breed some of these endangered poeciliids.

Within small populations, there is a real risk that genetic problems will arise. A potential threat to the long-term survival of livebearers is that isolated populations continue interbreeding, so that over time this has a deleterious effect on the reproductive potential of the species. This risk can sometimes prove to be unavoidable, however, as in the case of the Big Bend gambusia (*Gambusia gaigei*), whose very

⊕ A number of livebearers have very limited distributions. The Big Bend gambusia (*Gambusia gaigei*) seen here is currently one of the most endangered species.

future hung on the survival of a single female back in 1957. This Texan species, occurring near Boquillas in the Big Bend National Park, was rescued from its only known surviving locality in the Graham Ranch Warm Springs. Originally it was recorded in the Boquillas Spring itself, but this dried up by 1954.

Attempts to translocate specimens within the park had failed, and this left just a solitary female and two male fish of this species alive in aquariums. Luckily, the female bred successfully, and the resulting offspring were then transferred to a pool. It had been thought that the Big Bend gambusia faced competition from the western mosquito fish (*G. affinis*), but remarkably a leak in the holding pool revealed differences in habitat that allowed two such similar fish to coexist in the same area.

Big Bend gambusia were found to have colonized this running water, which had created a stream. However, they were not found in the adjacent still, stagnant water created by a beaver dam, which proved to be the favored habitat of the western mosquito fish instead. The distribution of the Big Bend gambusia increased during the winter of 1983, when the heavy rainfall carried some individuals from the original pond farther afield into another pool that had previously been home to its relative. Habitat changes here—notably the uncontrolled incursion of bulrushes (*Typha* spp.)—had helped to stabilize the water temperature at the more constant level preferred by the Big Bend gambusia. The additional throughflow from the leaking dike also appears to have been very important for this species.

In spite of the inevitably close genetic relationship between all the surviving Big Bend gambusia, these fish are nevertheless thriving as far as can be ascertained, certainly to the extent that they have displaced western mosquito fish in this habitat. Even so, they remain vulnerable during cold winters. With the world's climate patterns changing significantly as the result of global warming, even minor shifts in both rainfall and temperature may have serious consequences for populations of livebearers with localized distributions. Their future survival cannot be guaranteed.

A sad ending

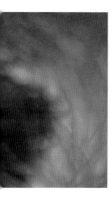

A salutary warning of what can happen is provided by the case of another livebearer from this region, the Amistad gambusia (*Gambusia amistadensis*). It was in April 1968 that an ichthyologist collected some of these fish from the Goodenough Spring, in Val Verde County, Texas. A further visit by another biologist occurred in August, just as the spring was swamped by the rise of the Amistad Reservoir. This appeared to mark the end of the species in the wild.

Stock from a breeding group in Austin was transferred to Dexter, and with two separate captive populations it appeared that the future for the Amistad gambusia was reasonably secure, even if its original habitat had disappeared. However, this created a difficulty in choosing suitable sites for reintroduction purposes. Worse still was that the fact that the waters that had created the Goodenough Spring were now flowing into existing streams close to the town of Del Rio, rather than establishing new channels. Unfortunately, these streams were already the habitat of another rare gambusia, *G. speciosa*, while the only other possible link back to the original stream was across the border in Mexico.

Critical delays ensued while planning studies involving the *G. speciosa* population and invertebrates in these streams were carried out, prior to the intended reintroduction program. This was to prove disastrous for the Amistad gambusia however, because both of the breeding colonies died out, and the species became extinct in 1984.

CHAPTER 2

The Different Groups

The tremendous popularity of livebearers means that if you visit virtually any tropical fish store you are likely to find a selection drawn from guppies, swordtails, platies, and mollies. These species all rank among the most popular tropical fish in the world, thanks partly to the development of colorful domestic strains in each case.

If the wild type of livebearers appeals to you, however, it may be much harder to track down suitable aquarium stock. You may need to seek out a specialist store, or search the Internet in order to find breeders of such fish. In some cases, you may have to be patient in order to acquire unrelated stock for breeding purposes, perhaps adding your name to a waiting list.

Joining a specialist livebearer group can be helpful in this respect, not just in terms of making contacts and acquiring stock, but also in keeping you up to date with the latest developments in the world of livebearers. This may even allow you to take part in study and collecting trips, enabling you to see the natural habitats of such fish at first hand. There is no doubt that in future years breeders of livebearers will have an increasingly important role to play in working with aquatic institutions to set up more captive breeding projects to conserve wild populations.

As the domestication of fish such as guppies has occurred, so there has been increasing interest in standardizing their appearance for exhibition purposes. Almost inevitably, it is a time-consuming task to develop ornamental strains of fish that display the desired characteristics of coloration and fin type. Such lines are carefully cherished by specialist breeders, and the individuals are far removed from the colorful mass-produced guppies that are now reared on fish farms around the globe in huge numbers.

While you may find some particularly attractive guppies among the assortment in your local aquatic store, if you are looking to establish a recognizable strain, then you will almost inevitably need to turn to a specialist breeder in this field. Here again, it helps to be informed about the fish that are winning. Even if you cannot visit such shows yourself, you should be able to follow them through reports in aquatic magazines and Internet postings, and can then gain a clear idea of the leading bloodlines. It is then relatively simple to make contact with the breeders, and it helps if you can arrange to visit and pick up your own fish.

Be prepared that such fish will be much more expensive than their typical pet store counterparts, because you are buying into the bloodline. In this respect, it is a bit like the difference between choosing a racehorse of proven pedigree and an ordinary horse. You may have to be patient, simply because the supply of quality potential show-winning fish is inevitably restricted as only a small number in any batch of fry is suitable.

● Many livebearers, such as these red tuxedo platies (*Xiphophorus maculatus* var.), show to best effect when kept in schools of the same variety.

MAKING CHOICES

Age considerations

As a result of the breeding behavior of many livebearers such as guppies, it is preferable to obtain young fish, even if they are not fully colored. Otherwise, although you may purchase an attractive pair with well-matched coloration, the likelihood is that the female may have mated before, and as a result your chosen male will not be the father of her progeny. Exhibition breeders of these fish rear the females separately, so they can be certain that they are virgin females when placing them with their chosen mates.

Another point to bear in mind when purchasing livebearers from traditional aquatic outlets is that in contrast to other, more expensive, fish such as discus (*Symphysodon* spp.), the guppies and other popular livebearers will typically be adults of unknown age. Since the lifespan of these fish can be relatively short, often not extending for more than a couple of years, they are unlikely to live for very long in your aquarium. Instead, it is their offspring that is likely to be there longer. Generally, buying younger individuals will represent a better investment over the longer term.

Health matters

The intensive commercial rearing of guppies and other livebearers for the aquarium trade in some parts of the world has seen changes in husbandry practices that have raised concerns about the overall health of fish from certain sources. The use of hormones, which can cause an improvement in the coloration of fish, and the administration of soluble antibiotics to damp down any risk of disease are controversial practices in the industry, and are blamed by some for weakening commercial strains of livebearers. It is therefore important to know the origins of the fish you are offered, for while they might look healthy in the store, they could succumb readily to minor infections, especially if they are ultimately mixed with established fish. This is because even the cleanest tank contains potentially harmful microbes, which while having no effect on healthy fish may cause problems with those that have depressed immune systems.

Never rush the purchase of fish. It is a good idea to pick a time when the store is likely to be quiet, so that you can concentrate on watching the aquarium occupants properly without being distracted by other people. Since many piscine ailments are spread through aquarium water, it is important to focus not only on the particular fish that appeal to you, but also on all the other tank occupants. Having just set up your aquarium, the last thing you want is to introduce any diseases that may then be difficult to eliminate. If any fish appear sick, are hanging in the water at a strange angle, have obvious difficulty in swimming, show abnormal spots on their bodies, or are particularly thin, then you should go elsewhere.

Healthy livebearers are generally lively, active fish, capable of swimming without difficulty, although some of the more ornate, corpulent fancy varieties—notably the balloon molly—may encounter difficulties in this respect. Otherwise, swimming problems may be a reflection of a disorder afflicting the swim bladder (the fish's organ of buoyancy), for which there is no effective cure. Any exaggeration in form can also create problems, and in the case of livebearers with more elaborate fins, be they fancy guppies or sailfin mollies, these should be checked carefully for signs of any damage. Ragged fins may be a reflection of poor environmental conditions and can predispose the fish to further infections. In mild cases of fin damage the fish should recover without problems, although the prognosis should be much more guarded where there are signs of fungus present. This usually shows up as a

◑ Be suspicious of any livebearers which swim at an abnormal angle in the water. This is an orange-tailed goodeid (*Xenotoca eiseni*) that proved to have a swim bladder problem (see page 118).

white haloed effect around the site of the injury, and will therefore be quite apparent on what are usually translucent fins in the case of livebearers.

Final checks

When you have decided which fish appeal to you, ask for them to be caught. Where all the fish appear to be identical, however—as in the case of a tank of black mollies—you will probably find it difficult to be selective. Sexing adult livebearers is not especially difficult in most cases. Males are usually smaller and may be more brightly colored. They are also recognizable by the structure of their anal fin, which has evolved into a rudimentary copulatory organ, known as a

gonopodium. Sexing young livebearers is correspondingly harder, simply because both sexes have similar anal fins at this stage—it takes several months for this feature to develop, depending on the species. Male mollies and swordtails, for example, may not be distinguishable on this basis until they are over nine months old.

Once the fish have been netted and transferred to a plastic bag, you should check them more carefully. You will be able to see any injury to the body or the fins far more easily at this range. Always be sure to look at both sides of the fishes' bodies. Check they have an eye on each side of the head (development abnormalities may

> ### FRESHWATER OR BRACKISH CONDITIONS?
>
> **One particular aspect of management that is especially significant is the type of water the fish are to be kept in. Brackish surroundings may make it less likely that the fish will develop fungal disease. But whatever the water, establish the required conditions carefully so that you can minimize the stress on the fish once they are in your care. You can then make any necessary adjustments gradually.**

⊕ Mollies are very prone to the parasitic disease known as "ich" or white spot, which spreads readily through the water.

result in fish occasionally having only one eye). Don't worry if you see a livebearer female with a dark spot visible on the sides of her body, as this is an indication that she will shortly give birth. However, you need to bear in mind that she may abort her offspring as a result of stress through being caught and moved at this stage.

The fish should be bagged individually, especially in the case of species that are likely to be aggressive, such as male swordtails (*Xiphophorus helleri*). Even mollies may fight seriously on just a short trip when several are confined in a relatively small bag, and this stress enhances the likelihood of subsequent health problems. The bags themselves contain relatively little water in any case, as they are topped up with oxygen to sustain the fish while they are travelling.

The plastic bag should be placed inside a dark paper bag as this will serve to calm the fish. Take the fish straight home, ensuring that the bag doesn't tip over and that nothing falls on top of it. You should also keep the fish out of the sun by carefully placing the bag on the floor of the car, possibly behind one of the front seats. Provided they are packed and transported carefully, livebearers can be moved long distances without worry in spite of their small size—consignments are often sent from one side of the U.S. to the other by air without problems.

BE PATIENT!

Only choose or arrange to collect the fish once you have set up your aquarium. Even in the case of a plug-in tank, which has all the components in place, it really is a good idea to have it set up and running properly for a few days beforehand. You can then make any small adjustments to the heater, for example, to regulate the water temperature, and allow the plants to settle down before introducing the fish. Most importantly perhaps, you can add a beneficial bacterial culture to start the filter bed, which means that water conditions during the critical early stages should be more favorable for the fish once they are introduced.

When you arrive home with the fish, do not simply tip them out of the bag into their new quarters. Instead, float the bag carefully on the surface of the tank for about 15 minutes or so to allow the water temperature inside the bag to reach that of the aquarium. You can then transfer the fish carefully, removing them from the bag with a small net. Finally, lift out the bag and tip the water away—this will avoid introducing potentially contaminated water from the fishes' previous aquarium.

It will take a day or so for the fish to settle in their new surroundings. To help them do so it is a good idea to keep the lights off during this period, particularly in the case of nervous species such as wrestling halfbeaks (*Dermogenys pusillus*), which could injure themselves by swimming wildly around the aquarium. Equally, the fish are unlikely to display much interest in food during this period, and any provided is likely to go to waste and will effectively pollute the water before the filter is working at its optimum efficiency. It is therefore not a good idea to feed the fish for the first day, and subsequently it is important to offer them only what they will eat within a few moments, for the same reason.

CLASSIFICATION

The way in which fish are grouped does not differ from that used for other animals, or indeed plants. Their classification operates through a series of ranks, which become more specific as one progresses through the classificatory tree to its higher branches. The science underlying classification (known as taxonomy) is not static, however, and in a number of cases it is controversial. As a result, there can be disagreements over the divisions, and this is reflected in the different names used. This is especially true in the case of genus and species

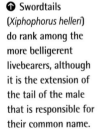

⊙ Swordtails (*Xiphophorus helleri*) do rank among the more belligerent livebearers, although it is the extension of the tail of the male that is responsible for their common name.

names, where individual populations may be involved. The example below left of the four-eyed fish shows how the system works.

Members of the order Cyprinodontiformes are known as toothcarps, and are traditionally divided into two groupings based on their method of reproduction. The egg-laying members of this order are described as killifishes, whereas those that give birth to live young comprise the livebearers, which are the subject of this book. The concept that this key difference in reproductive strategy is sufficient to separate these groups has, however, been challenged by some taxonomists in recent years, notably Lynne Parenti in 1981.

Anatomical studies currently underpin much of the existing taxonomy, with particular regard being paid to the structure of the gonopodium in livebearers. However, taxonomy is currently being revolutionized by the application of DNA technology to identify biochemical relationships in this field, so that further revisions at all levels are likely to be inevitable in the future.

What's in a name?

There are several key indicators that help to reveal where in the taxonomic tree a name fits. All the names of the livebearer orders terminate in the suffix "-iformes," while their family names end in "-idae." Order and family names also appear in Roman type and start with a capital letter. Genus names are always a single word that appears in italics, as in *Anableps*. Each genus is comprised of one or more species, and when referring to all species within the genus the abbreviation "spp." may appear after the name—for example, *Anableps* spp. refers to all three species within the *Anableps* genus.

The scientific names of species consist of two words: the first is the genus name beginning with a capital letter, while the second, given name, also in italic, starts

TAXONOMY
Kingdom: Animalia
Phylum: Chordata
Class: Actinopterygii
Order: Cyprinodontiformes
Suborder: Cyprinodontoidei
Superfamily: Poecilioidea
Family: Anablepidae
Subfamily: Anablepinae
Genus: *Anableps*
Species: *Anableps anableps;* *A. dowi; A. microlepis*

with a lower case letter. Although this is often said to be the fish's Latin name, this is not strictly correct as the names are not always of Latin origin or based on Latin. The word *anableps*, for example, comes from the Greek, and means "large eyes." Many scientific names do seek to describe particular features of the species in question, although they may incorporate the name of a person linked closely with the species. The generic description *Jenynsia*, for example, commemorates the name of Rev. L. Jenyns, a prominent and respected Victorian naturalist.

Sometimes there is a further level beyond that of the species' rank. This is known as the subspecies (abbreviated to "ssp."), and serves to distinguish between what are effectively isolated populations that clearly show signs of diverging from one another, and that consequently display recognizable and consistent differences. Subspecies are distinguished by the addition of a third name to that of the species. Where the specific name is repeated, this is referred to as the nominate race. This is not necessarily the most common form, however, but is simply the first to have been described. There are two recognized subspecies in the case of *Phallichthys amates*, for example. These are the merry widow (*Phallichthys amates amates*) found in southern Guatemala and northern Honduras, on the Atlantic side of Central America, with the larger, blue form known as the orange-dorsal livebearer (*P. a. pittieri*) occurring further south, from Nicaragua to Panama.

◑ The northerly subspecies of the merry widow (*Phallichthys amates amates*) can be distinguished from its southerly counterpart by its coloration and smaller size.

Common names can be confusing, as illustrated by the case of this goodea which has three English common names: elfin goodeid, two-lined skiffia, and blackfin goodeid. Scientific nomenclature gives each species a unique name, however, which in this case is *Skiffia bilineata*.

When a new species is discovered, it can only be officially accorded its name once a specimen has been lodged in a recognized museum collection and a detailed description of it has been published in a scientific journal. This is known as the type specimen. Color varieties are not considered by taxonomists as separate species. Instead, they are simply identified by the addition of the abbreviation "var." after the name of the species. The same applies in cases where the fin structure has been modified by selective breeding.

Defining a species is not an easy task, certainly in the case of livebearers. In theory, although members of the same genus are closely related and may occasionally hybridize together, they should not be able to produce fertile offspring. In contrast, subspecies can pair together without such problems. As an example, this line of argument was taken in the decision to recognize the eastern mosquito fish (*Gambusia holbrooki*) as a separate species from the western mosquito fish (*G. affinis*) rather than a subspecies. When these two discernibly similar forms were mated together, they produced a high incidence of dead and deformed offspring. Even so, this guideline is not infallible, as shown by the four-eyed fish (*Anableps anableps*), where the gonopodium of the male fish may be deviated either to the right or left. This means that they can only mate with females of the alternate configuration, but there is no attempt to group these fish separately based on their external reproductive organs.

While a scientific name should be universally consistent, a fish may have one or more common names in each language. In some such cases, it can become unclear which species is actually being described. As an example, *Skiffia bilineata* is known both as the blackfin goodeid and as the two-lined skiffia, not to mention its other English name—the elfin! Many of the lesser-known livebearers do not actually have a common name, however, and may simply be described under their scientific name, or a corrupted version of it. Girardinus is the common name accorded to a specific species in this genus—*Girardinus metallicus*.

Members of all of the four families—Goodeidae, Anablepidae (which now also incorporates the Jenynsiidae), Poeciliidae, and Hemirhamphidae—that are usually considered to be the traditional livebearing fish are discussed in the following pages of this chapter. More detailed coverage of requirements of the most popular species is the subject of Chapter 7.

FAMILY GOODEIDAE:
GOODEIDS OR MEXICAN LIVEBEARERS

As their common name suggests, these fish are restricted to Mexico, where they are found especially in the states of Michoacán and Jalisco. Within their highland distribution they have evolved into diverse forms that have colonized particular habitats—a phenomenon known as adaptive radiation. The body shape of these fish reveals much. Those that live in pools and slow-flowing stretches of water have broader bodies than their counterparts living in upland streams, where a sleek, streamlined body shape makes swimming easier, especially when aided by a powerful caudal fin. For many years, goodeids have not been especially popular with fishkeepers, but there are now signs of a growing interest in this family.

Allodontichthys

The four species in the genus are all quite small, averaging just under 2in (5cm) in length, with less of a size difference between the sexes than in other genera. These goodeids can be highly aggressive toward each other, as in the case of A. hubbsi, and so their quarters must include rockwork and similar items that can provide retreats. They are not well known in aquarist circles, and are slow to reproduce. Females may carry the young for two months or so after mating, and brood size is consequently small. A maximum of about 20 offspring is produced, but more typically the number of fry is in single figures. A. hubbsi and A. polylepsis are under threat in the wild.

➊ Many common names refer to the appearance of a fish or its behavior, or may even derive from its scientific name. This is girardinus (*Girardinus metallicus*), also called the metallic top minnow.

➍ Orange darter goodeid (*Allodontichthys polylepsis*). This is the latest addition to the genus.

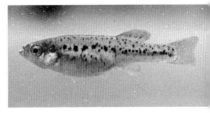

● Regal goodeid
(*Allotoca regalis*).
The body shape
of females of this
genus often becomes
distorted when they
are gravid.

Alloophorus

This genus comprises two species, both from Mexico, which are virtually unrecorded in the aquarium hobby. They are relatively large fish, with females reaching a size of nearly 5in (12.5cm) in the case of *A. robustus*. The smaller *A. regalis* has been recorded in both swampy areas and slow-flowing water where there is thick algal growth on the rocks. The head shape of *Alloophorus* goodeids is characteristically rounded, with a large mouth that betrays their predatory instincts. Both dorsal and anal fins are spaced well back on the body, toward the caudal fin. Broods may consist of over 60 young, born approximately two months after mating. The young need to be separated from the adult fish as soon as possible, or they are likely to be eaten by the adults.

Allotoca

The precise number of species in this genus is unclear, not only because of taxonomic arguments but also as a result of fears that *A. maculata* may be extinct within its very limited range in the Santa Magdalena lagoon and Etzatlán in the Mexican state of Jalisco. This would rank almost as a coldwater species as the water temperature of its native habitats typically averages about 60°F (15.5°C). Other members of the genus can be maintained successfully in waters of 68–72°F (20–22°C). The golden bumblebee goodeid (*A. dugesii*) is the most commonly kept member of its genus, with the females lacking the yellow coloration seen in the male fish. Gravid females are ideally housed in a breeding tank until they give birth. It takes up to eight weeks after mating for the young to be produced, and as many as 76 have been recorded in a single brood.

● Butterfly goodeid
(*Ameca splendens*).
These fish are
so called because
of the shape of the
dorsal fin in males.

Ameca

This is a monotypic genus, which means that it is comprised of a single species, known as the butterfly goodeid (*A. splendens*). These fish were among the first members of the family to attract the attention of aquarists back in the 1970s. As with other goodeids from the Jalisco area of Mexico, they are quite happy in a range of water temperatures. In the aquarium

temperature changes should be made gradually, as would occur in the wild in response to the changing seasons. It may be that fluctuations in temperature play a part in conditioning these livebearers for breeding. Butterfly goodeids will thrive better if they are kept in groups rather than as odd pairs in community aquariums, when they are more likely to display aggressive tendencies toward their companions. Even so, care must be taken to ensure they are not overcrowded, as this will always trigger disagreements.

⬆ Polkadot goodeid (*Chapalichthys pardalis*). The specific name of this fish— 'pardalis '—alludes to its spotted, leopardlike patterning.

Ataeniobius

The single member of this genus, known as the blue-tailed goodeid (*A. toweri*) is sometimes regarded as a member of the *Goodea* genus (*see* page 33). Occurring close to the city of Río Verde in Mexico's San Luis Potosí state, this goodeid faces an uncertain future. Like other members of the family it has a limited distribution, and is found only in the Media Luna canal, which is fed by warm-water springs from two caves. The slightly sulfurous water here is thought to afford the fish some protection against fungus and other infections that develop readily in the confines of an aquarium. Unfortunately, as its natural habitat is being used increasingly by the growing human population, so the numbers of these fish are declining. Some breeding successes have been recorded, however, with females producing as many as 37 fry. The females give birth about eight weeks after mating, and the young goodeids grow quite slowly, sometimes not attaining sexual maturity until they are seven months old.

Chapalichthys

An interesting feature of males of this genus is that they have a vertical yellow band on their caudal fin, which disappears if they are

kept in suboptimal conditions, when the pH reading of the water drops below neutral. *Chapalichthys* is a small genus, comprised of two or possibly three species. As to their appearance, these goodeids are not dissimilar to *Ameca splendens* (*see* above), which also has a yellow band evident on its caudal fin. They do best in relatively cool water at 64–75°F (18–24°C), with some seasonal variation as they encounter in their Mexican homeland. They are ideally housed in a well-planted single-species-only setup. Females give birth to quite small numbers of fry, with broods usually comprising 10–20 young. It can be difficult in some cases to tell that the females of these livebearers are gravid. Beware of keeping *Chapalichthys* goodeids, which average around 2.4in (6cm), in the company of smaller companions as they are likely to harass them.

Characodon

These goodeids are the most northerly occurring in Mexico, and are found in the province of Durango in relatively still stretches of water. There are three surviving species, plus one other, christened *C. garmani*, which is known just from a single specimen and is feared to be extinct. They are high backed, with dorsal and anal fins positioned relatively close to the caudal fin. As their distribution suggests, they can be found in water where the temperature is as low as 64°F (18°C), although a figure of about 75°F (24°C) suits them better in aquarium surroundings. They feed largely on algae, but will also take live food. Unfortunately, characodons have proved to be quite aggressive toward each other and so need to be kept in surroundings where there is plenty of cover. They are also fairly shy by nature. Females generally have quite small broods, comprising on average 10–20 fry, but on occasion nearly 60 have been recorded in a single brood. The gestation period lasts approximately eight weeks.

Girardinichthys

The two species comprising this genus are found in waters in the vicinity of Mexico City itself, and they now face an uncertain future as development is taking place within their area of distribution. They are better represented than some goodeids within the aquarium hobby, however, giving hope for their long term survival. As with a number of other related species, best results have been recorded when they are kept in water temperatures that correspond closely to those of their natural environment—typically 68–72°F (20–22°C), although they may survive significantly colder conditions. The range of one species, the amarillo (*G. viviparus*), used to include Chapultepec Park, where winter frosts occasionally occurred. Their aquarium needs to be well planted, and the water chemistry kept mildly alkaline and medium-hard. These goodeids are omnivorous in their feeding habits, but vegetable-based flaked food should always feature prominently in their diet. Twenty or so fry are born after a gestation period lasting approximately two months.

Goodea

There is considerable disagreement among taxonomists about whether all members of this group are simply subspecies of *G. atripinnis*, or if they should be accorded individual specific status, which would create as many as three separate species. Not all the forms are represented within the aquarium hobby in any case. Silvery coloration tends to distinguish these relatively large goodeids, and wild-caught females have been documented as attaining a length

◐ Amarillo (*Girardinichthys viviparus*) giving birth. The anal fin of these goodeids is noticeably large.

of nearly 8in (20cm). Their housing needs to be correspondingly spacious. As with other goodeids, the females nourish their offspring during the gestation period, but in this case the trophotaeniae (cords that provide nutrients to the developing fry) are surprisingly small and shaped more like rosettes.

Hubbsina

The single species in this genus, *H. turneri*, which occurs in the Mexican states of Michoacán and Guanajuato, is little studied although fears have been expressed about its survival. The larger females grow to about 2.6in (6.5cm) in length, while the males average around 2in (5cm) and have a less obvious pattern of spotting on their bodies. They have a large dorsal fin, which is virtually rectangular in shape, extending along the top of the body to the caudal peduncle. It has proved possible to maintain these goodeids in hard, alkaline water heated to about 77°F (25°C), but breeding

details do not appear to have been documented to date. Feeding may be problematic as one group of *Hubbsina* was found to eat live food avidly but refused all dry diets.

Ilyodon

The elongated, streamlined body shape of these goodeids indicates that they are powerful swimmers and hence inhabit rivers rather than more sedentary stretches of water. The number of recognized species in this genus is again controversial, varying from two to four. They are thought to be in a transitional phase of evolution—the form described as *I. xantusi* is considered to be a broad-mouthed morph of *I. furcidens*, which often occurs alongside it. Their center of distribution is in rivers flowing from the southern slope of the Mesa Central in Mexico, westward in the direction of the Pacific coast. These goodeids can be kept successfully within a temperature range of 64–79°F (18–26°C), in slightly hard and alkaline water. They are quite straightforward to feed, being omnivorous in their habits. Females typically produce between 20 and 35 fry after a gestation period lasting about two months.

Skiffia

The four members of this genus are all relatively small in size, the females averaging about 2.4in (6cm) in length and the males around 1.6in (4cm). They can instantly be separated from other goodeids by the uneven appearance of their dorsal fin, which has led to them being dubbed sawfin goodeids. Their distribution encompasses the Mexican provinces of Jalisco, Guanajuato, and Michoacán. The fry are produced about eight weeks after mating in relatively small broods, often ranging from as few as five up to 20. *Skiffia francesae* was assessed as "EW"–extinct in the wild–by the IUCN in 1996.

Xenoophorus

This is another monotypic genus, occurring in the Mexican state of San Luis Potosí. *X. captivus* occurs in algal-ridden waters, largely free of other vegetation, and not surprisingly algae feature prominently in the diet. Their actual coloration is quite variable, although males can always easily be identified by their larger dorsal and anal fins. Anywhere between 10 and 30 fry may be born, with gestation taking about 55 days. Already at birth, the fish will measure over 0.5in (1.2cm) in length. Unlike many livebearers, there is no need to transfer the gravid female to a separate breeding setup, because the adult fish are usually unlikely to prey on the fry.

◑ The gold sailfin goodeid (*Skiffia francesae*) is possibly extinct in the wild, after having only been described for the first time in 1978. Thankfully, there are still captive-bred strains in several countries.

⬆ Green goodeid (*Xenoophorus captivus*). Vegetable matter is important in the diet of this fish.

Xenotaenia

The single species in this genus, *X. resolanae*, is named after the Río Resolana in the Mexican state of Jalisco, where it was discovered in 1946. The waters where it has since been observed are full of algae and also choked with hornwort (*Ceratophyllum*), which can be cultivated in an aquarium. These goodeids feed mainly on vegetable matter, but will also eat live foods. The water temperature should be maintained around 75°F (24°C). Breeding details are similar to those of *Xenoophorus* (see above). An interesting observation is that these goodeids may seek to attack companions of similar or larger size, often nipping their fins, but will ignore their own young or smaller fish sharing their quarters.

Xenotoca

The three members of the *Xenotoca* genus are all quite brightly colored compared with other goodeids, with the red-tailed goodeid (*X. eiseni*) ranking among the most widely kept members of the family. The dorsal fin that is set well back and especially prominent in males, while the mouth is small and undershot, the lower jaw protruding

⮕ Red-tailed goodeid (*Xenotoca eiseni*). The body shape of males changes as they grow older, as they develop a humped appearance.

beyond the upper. *Xenotoca* goodeids are very adaptable fish, being found in waters whose temperatures may vary seasonally from just 59°F up to 91°F (15–33°C). They can also be encountered in a wide range of habitats, from rivers to ditches, although usually these are full of vegetation. They take a varied diet, and females typically produce 25–30 fry after a gestation period of about eight weeks.

Zoogoneticus

This is another monotypic genus, whose sole member, *Z. quitzeoensis*, is named after Lake Cuitzeo in the Mexican state of Michoacán, where it is found. It also occurs in the neighboring states of Jalisco and Guanajuato. There are three distinctive color morphs that have been described from separate parts of the species' range, also differing in size. The yellow variant is the smallest, the red form slightly larger, and the orange morph is the biggest. Size differences are relatively slight. None of these goodeids is large—on average, males measure up to 2in (5cm) and females reach 3in (7.5cm) in length. The water temperature is quite critical to their well-being, and should be maintained at about 77°F (25°C). The water should be hard and slightly alkaline. Females produce relatively few fry—often no more than 15– 55 days following mating. Rearing the young in tanks that are rich in algae seems to improve both their growth rate and coloration.

FAMILY ANABLEPIDAE: FOUR-EYES AND RELATED SPECIES

This family of fish, from parts of Central and South America, is the smallest within the livebearer category, comprising three genera and five species, each with deviated genitalia.

Anableps

The three species forming this unmistakable genus all have a similar lifestyle, frequently swimming just below the surface with their eyes partly protruding into the air above. This allows them to spot insects

⬆ It may be that the crescent goodeid turns out to be a separate species from *Z. quitzeoensis*. It has been given the descriptions *Zoogoneticus* sp. "Crescent", and tentatively, *Z. tequila*.

in their vicinity without difficulty. They are found largely in brackish waters, with *A. microlepis* also occurring in a marine environment on occasions, at the mouth of the Amazon River. The most northerly occurring of the *Anableps* spp. is *A. dowi*, which ranges as far as Río Tehuantepec in Oaxaca, Mexico, and has also been reported off the coast there and in various Pacific localities such as Cutuco in El Salvador and Puntarenas in Costa Rica. The requirements of these species are not significantly different from those of *A. anableps* itself, which is the most commonly kept form. However, *A. dowi* females can grow up to 4.7in (12cm) bigger than *A. anableps*, reaching 13.7in (35cm) overall, and this difference needs to be reflected in the size of their accommodations. All species should be kept in brackish water.

Jenynsia

The only member of its genus, *J. lineata* can be distinguished from other members of the family in that the tubular gonopodium of male fish is not covered by scales. Just as in the case of related genera, however, the gonopodium itself is deviated, as are the genital openings of female fish, so they must be suitably aligned for pairing to be successful. These fish inhabit shallow, coastal lagoons where there is widespread algal growth, which helps to provide them with vital nutrients. Studies suggest that it is more important to keep these fish in aquariums where there is an extensive algal covering, even without salt, rather than in brackish water alone. Their distribution extends from southern Brazil to northern Argentina.

Oxyzygonectes

The single species in this genus, known as Dowe's minnow and described scientifically as both *O. dowi* and *O. dovii*, is thought to provide a link between the livebearing toothcarps and their egg-laying relatives, the killifishes. The species' distribution extends along the Pacific coast of Panama and Costa Rica in Central America. Dowe's minnows are of a silvery color, with a dorsal fin that is positioned almost adjacent to the caudal, at the rear of their streamlined body. The head in particular is narrow in width, and the eyes appear to be correspondingly large.

Dowe's minnows are not widely kept, partly because (contrary to the suggestion inherent in their name) they are large fish, with individuals growing up to 13.7in (35cm) in length. In addition, they need to be housed in groups, which means that they require a spacious tank setup. This should contain brackish water, corresponding to the coastal lagoons that form their natural habitat. Feeding is not difficult, as they will eat a wide range of foodstuffs. What sets these fish apart from almost all the others covered in this book, however, is their reproductive habits. Nevertheless, the fact that males have an obvious anal papilla, which is deviated to the right or left as with the other fish in this family, is the reason for its inclusion in this taxon.

Female Dowe's minnows will spawn among plants, rather than giving birth to live young. They will even use spawning mops provided for killifishes, which allows their eggs to be transferred easily to a separate aquarium, where the young can be reared safely. Females, recognizable by their transparent rather than yellowish fins, may lay 40 eggs or more at a single spawning. The resulting fry can be raised without problems on fry food and brine shrimp nauplii.

FAMILY POECILIIDAE: GUPPIES AND RELATED SPECIES

This family contains the most popular livebearers, so far as the aquarium hobby is concerned. Once again, however, not all the species included under this heading do in fact produce live young, with a small proportion laying eggs instead. Since it was first proposed in 1895, this family has been subjected to a number of taxonomic revisions.

Alfaro

The two species that form this genus are found in an area of Central America extending from southern Guatemala to Panama.

⬇ Knife livebearer (*Alfaro cultratus*). The sharp keels of these fish, which have been likened to the blade of a knife in shape, are a very obvious feature.

They are popularly known as knifefish because of their body shape, the underside of their body resembling the blade of a knife. *Alfaro* is regarded as one of the more primitive genera, thanks to the structure of the male's gonopodium, which is also relatively long. The extensive ventral fins associated with male knifefish are used as an aid to courtship, being employed to caress the female's head at this stage. The orange knife livebearer (*A. huberi*) has gained a reputation for being particularly difficult to keep successfully, and well-filtered, moving water is essential for its well-being. Young knifefish are slow to mature and may not breed for the first time until they are a year old.

Belonesox

These fish were discovered in 1860 and given a generic name derived from the Greek word *belone*, which translates as "arrowhead," and *esox*, the Latin word for pike, a good description of the appearance of these livebearers. There is only one recognized species, *B. belizanus*, found in parts of Central America. Young fish display dark horizontal bands on their bodies, which may help to provide them with camouflage, although in aquarium surroundings smaller individuals should not be mixed with larger fish as they are likely to be eaten by them. Ranking among the most predatory of all livebearers, these fish may be reluctant to take inert foodstuffs in the confines of an aquarium, and as a consequence some breeders offer them unwanted young guppies. This beak-mouthed, saber toothed species has been in the hobby for 100 years.

○ Piketop minnow (*Belonesox belizanus*). The almost horizontal top line on the body is a characteristic feature of these highly predatory livebearers.

Brachyrhaphis

The nine species in this genus occur throughout Central America, on both the Pacific and Atlantic sides of the region. They often display a black diamondlike outline over their bodies and also usually show an area of black pigment on the anal fin. *Brachyrhaphis* spp. are relatively long bodied and also quite colorful, particularly in the case of the cardinal brachy (*B. roseni*). Unfortunately, they are also aggressive fish, with strong cannibalistic traits that can make breeding problematic. The gestation period lasts about a month, with 10 to 40 young being born depending on the species concerned. Small live foods such as brine shrimp nauplii are valuable for rearing purposes, and live foods such as midge larvae continue to feature in the diets of older individuals as well. *Brachyrhaphis* livebearers are found in both brackish and freshwater surroundings, and a typical water temperature of about 75°F (24°C) suits these fish well.

⊕ Cardinal brachy (*Brachyrhaphis roseni*). The distinctive red markings on the fins help to explain the common name of this species.

Carlhubbsia

The two species forming this genus occur in Mexico and Guatemala, where they are found in a wide variety of habitats, in water temperatures up to 86°F (30°C). *C. stuarti* is slightly smaller and yet more brightly colored than *C. kidderi*. Males grow up to 2in (5cm) and females may reach 2.4in (6cm) in the latter case, and it is also possible to distinguish between fish of Mexican and Guatemalan origins since the more southerly population has a prominent yellow area encircling the black spot present on its dorsal fin. Typical brood sizes in either case average 10 to 30 fry, which are born about a month after mating. Tanks that are densely covered with algae are ideal for rearing these young livebearers at first, and brine shrimp nauplii are valuable food at this stage. They will attain sexual maturity at about four months.

Cnesterodon

These small livebearers are found in southeastern parts of South America, specifically in parts of Bolivia, Brazil, Paraguay, Argentina, and Uruguay. The genus is now comprised of four species, two of which were identified for the first time in 1993. They are all quite similar in appearance, with males averaging about 1in (2.5cm) in length, while females are again larger, measuring up to 1.8in (4.5cm). *Cnesterodon* spp. are relatively plain in color, typically displaying a silvery sheen on their underparts. They are easy to maintain, however, in spite of their size, particularly in a relatively small aquarium. The water temperature here should be around 75°F (24°C). Their small mouths mean they must be offered food that they can swallow without difficulty. This can include flaked food and tiny live foods such as brine shrimp nauplii, and they will also browse on any algae growing in their aquarium. Their gestation period lasts just 24 days, the resulting brood comprising between five and 20 fry. The young fish may themselves be mature at three months.

Flexipenis

The single *Flexipenis* species, *F. vittatus*, is closed allied with members of the *Gambusia* genus, and is even incorporated into this genus by some taxonomists although it has not proved possible to hybridize these forms. This may be related in part to the fact that the copulatory organ of the male is both more flexible and shorter than in the case of *Gambusia* spp. *Flexipenis* is found in Mexico, ranging from the Río Pánuco region in Tamaulipas to Veracruz. It can be encountered in a range of habitats, from rivers to streams and ponds, and is quite adaptable as far as its aquarium needs go. A water temperature of 75–82°F (24–28°C) is ideal for these fish, and they will eat a variety of foods. Males can be most easily distinguished from females by their smaller size, averaging about 1.8in (4.5cm) in length. The

⊙ The black-seam mosquito fish (*Flexipenis vittatus*) ranks among the most attractive of all wild livebearers, thanks to its highly distinctive coloration.

fry, numbering 15 to 30, are born after a gestation period of about six weeks, and will be capable of breeding from the age of four months onward.

● *Gambusia puncticulata*. The taxonomy of this particular species is confused, and may include a number of other Central American *Gambusia* forms, which were previously accorded specific status in their own right.

Gambusia

This is a large genus comprising more than 30 species, which are generally all described as mosquito fish because of their propensity for eating the aquatic life stages of this insect. As a result, they have become valued as a means of biological control for killer diseases such as malaria and yellow fever, which are spread through the bites of female mosquitoes. These fish have a wide natural area of distribution, from the Eastern Seaboard southward via Central America to northern parts of Colombia. They are represented on some Caribbean islands, and have also been introduced deliberately to various parts of the world well outside their natural range. In addition, the group includes a number of species that have restricted areas of distribution and are under threat in the wild. These include *G. amistadensis*, which was confined to the warm waters of Goodenough Spring in Val Verde County, Texas, but is now probably extinct (see page 19).

Girardinus

Seven members of this genus are found on the Caribbean island of Cuba, while the eighth occurs on the small adjoining landmass known as the Isle of Pines. Unfortunately, in spite of being quite easy to maintain and breed in aquarium surroundings, these livebearers are rarely available. The species that is most often encountered is *G. metallicus*, to the extent that it is often described simply as girardinus. Males are significantly smaller, measuring as little as 1.1in (3cm) in some cases, while females are usually at least twice as large. As with other members of the genus, *G. metallicus* is not brightly colored, although black markings caused by melanism are quite common on the body of males.

Girardinus itself inhabits a wide range of environments throughout Cuba, and has been kept in aquariums since 1906. These fish, as with related species, will thrive at temperatures of 72–77°F (22–25°C), with a pH around neutral and in relatively hard water. They are generally peaceful and lively aquarium occupants, preferring a tank that includes floating plants as well as others set in the substrate. Girardinus are omnivorous in their feeding habits, and are likely to be cannibalistic toward their off-

⬆ Metallic top minnow (*Girardinus metallicus*). One of the most commonly available members of the genus.

spring. The female will produce a brood of between 10 and 40 about four weeks after mating.

Heterandria

The range of this genus extends from the southern U.S., down to Guatemala in Central America. One of the best-known members of the group is the mosquito fish (*H. formosa*), which has a particularly interesting breeding cycle. The young fish in this case are nourished directly by their mother, which means that she must be provided with a nutritious diet if their development is to be unimpaired. She produces small broods very frequently, usually every few days. As they originate from the northern part of the genus's range, these fish should be kept in cooler surroundings over the winter months, at a water temperature around 61–64°F (16–18°C). Depending on the ambient room temperature, this may mean simply switching off the heater for this time, and subsequently increasing the temperature again gradually over several weeks, back up to 75°F (24°C) or so.

Heterophallus

The three species of livebearer in this genus are endemic to Mexico, ranging from Veracruz to Chiapas. They are closely related to *Gambusia*, but the males have a different gonopodium structure. The males are about 1in (2.5cm) long, with females typically 1.1–1.3in (3–3.5cm). The most common species kept in aquariums is *H. rachowi*, which naturally occurs in shallow, shady backwaters where there is dense aquatic vegetation. A well-planted aquarium, with the water maintained at around 81°F (27°C), will suit them best. They need a diet that includes small live foods as well as a vegetable flaked food. Under favorable conditions, females will give birth to between five and 20 offspring after an interval of 28 days following mating. The young are not persecuted by adult fish, especially where there is adequate cover.

Limia

All the 20-odd species forming this genus are to be found in the Caribbean region, specifically the Cayman Islands, Hispaniola, Cuba, and Jamaica, but are absent from the American mainland. Not all *Limia* spp. are present in the aquarium hobby, so their requirements are not fully known, but in general terms these livebearers prefer relatively warm water, typically around 77°F (25°C), with a pH reading between neutral and alkaline. The water chemistry itself is less significant, although extremes of hardness or softness should be avoided. A number of species such as *L. caymanensis*, which inhabits coastal lagoons, also prefer brackish water conditions, and live foods, especially brine shrimp nauplii, are important in their diet and for the successful rearing of their young. A number of species are quite colorful and often display speckled markings on their bodies.

Neoheterandria

The distribution of this genus extends from Panama to northwestern South America. The most commonly kept of the three species is now *N. elegans*, which is found in the Río Truando, Colombia. All are relatively small in size, with male fish averaging no more than 0.8in (2cm) long, while females may grow to 1in (2.5cm) in the case of *N. elegans*. They are attractively colored with a slender profile. The belly area is silvery, with a series of dark bands on the sides of the body, which is otherwise yellowish. Blue edging is apparent on the fins. Because of their size, these livebearers are best housed in a single-species aquarium. The temperature should be maintained

◑ Tiburon limia (*Limia tridens*). The coloration of these attractive Haitian livebearers can be quite variable.

at a figure of 75–82°F (24–28°C) and fine-leaved aquatic plants incorporated into their tank. They will browse on algae, and should be offered powdered vegetable flaked food as well as small live foods such as brine shrimp nauplii. Like the *Heterandria* spp., the females give birth to just one or two fry every few days. It is usually safe to rear the fry alongside the adult fish.

Phallichthys

All four of the species comprising this Central American genus have a distinctive dark line running across their eyes onto their cheeks. They are not brightly colored, although the merry widow subspecies (*P. amates amates*) is an attractive yellowish shade overall. Males grow to about 1.1in (3cm), while the larger females reach 2.8in (7cm) overall. They are not particularly difficult fish to keep as they occur in a wide variety of different habitats in the wild. A planted aquarium, where the water is maintained at around 77°F (25°C), is quite suitable. Males have a gonopodium that is deviated from the midline, as in some other livebearing fish. The young are born as early as three weeks after mating, although they are small at this stage, typically measuring 0.16in (4mm). Broods may be comprised of 50 or more fry. If they are reared on special fry food they'll grow quickly, and be mature by three months old.

Phalloceros

The markings of the fish that forms this genus are remarkably varied, and this has given rise to a wide range of common names,

🔽 Merry widow (*Phallichthys amates*), a livebearer that gets its name because of the black stripe running through the eye.

including spotted livebearer, one-spot livebearer, and golden spotted livebearer. Some individuals display a more blotched rather than spotted patterning. *P. caudimaculatus* is found in South America, specifically in Paraguay, Uruguay, and southern Brazil. Some populations occur in brackish water, and at the time of purchase (if not before) it is important to discover how such fish are being kept, so that you can provide the corresponding conditions.

Males measure approximately 1.2in (3cm), while females grow up to 2in (5cm) in length. As they originate from a southerly latitude, a water temperature of 64–75°F (18–24°C) is recommended for these livebearers; this can be cooled toward the lower end of the range for a month or so during the winter. After a gestation period of up to six weeks, the females will give birth to as many as 80 offspring.

Phalloceros caudimaculatus. The markings of these particular fish are highly individual.

Phalloptychus

This genus is named after the male's curved gonopodium. Both species occur in South America, specifically Brazil, Paraguay, and Uruguay. They are small fish, the males averaging about 1in (2.5cm) in length and the females measuring about 1.6in (4cm). Only the striped millions fish (*P. januarius*) is likely to be encountered in aquarist circles at present. The other species, *P. eigenmanni*, was kept for a time during 1981 in its native Brazil, but there seem to be no other aquarium records for these particular fish. Brackish water conditions are recommended for the striped millions fish, as well as a water temperature of around 77°F (25°C). Females give birth to their brood of 10 to 30 fry over the course of seven to 10 days, rather than all at once. Small live foods are recommended for rearing purposes. These fish are so called because they can be very prolific (the females give birth every 24 days or so) and are also encountered in large numbers in the wild.

Phallotorynus

The gonopodium of males of the two species forming this genus is branched, and is sometimes described as having an antlerlike shape.

These small fish are found in southeastern parts of Brazil as well as Paraguay. They are virtually unknown at present in aquarist circles, but their care would probably not differ significantly from that of similar genera, including *Cnesterodon* and *Phalloptychus* (see page 42 and 47). Again, the water temperature should be allowed to fall over the winter period.

Poecilia

By far the best known of the livebearing toothcarp genera, *Poecilia* is a controversial genus among ichthyologists. This is because it comprises a number of species—including the guppy (*P. reticulata*)—that could be classified separately. *Limia* is now more commonly separated out as a genus from this grouping, rather than being accorded the rank of subgenus, as sometimes is *Micropoecilia*. However, there are certain features that serve to identify members of the *Poecilia* genus. For example, the pelvic fins of males aid the positioning and movement of the gonopodium during mating. Males of almost all *Poecilia* spp. also have a distinctive fleshy palp at the tip of this organ.

It is not easy to generalize about the care of members of this genus, because of the wide diversity of habitats in which they are found. There are approximately 24 recognized species within this exclusively American genus, whose natural distribution ranges from the southeastern states right across Central America down into central and eastern parts of South America. As a means of clarifying the relationships in this group, the genus itself has therefore been split into three different subgenera.

The *Lebistes* subgenus includes the popular guppy, *Poecilia* (*Lebistes*) *reticulata*, and five other, less well-known species. This grouping also incorporates the attractive species sometimes grouped as *Micropoecilia*. Perhaps the best known is the black-banded

◗ Blond cobra guppy (*Poecilia reticulata*). Male fish are especially colorful.

poecilia (sometimes classified as *M. picta*), which requires brackish water. These fish have proved quite difficult to breed, although tanks covered in algae offer the best likelihood of success.

The *Mollienisia* subgenus, which is the most recent subdivision to be proposed, includes well-established aquarium favorites such as the sailfin molly, *Poecilia (Mollienisia) latipinna*. Some taxonomists consider it to be synonymous with *Poecilia* as a subgeneric description. In contrast, members of the third subgenus, *Pamphorichthys*, are not widely kept in aquariums. They are confined to parts of South America.

Poeciliopsis

This is another large genus, comprising more than 20 species that are sometimes divided into two subgenera—*Poeciliopsis* and *Aulophallus*—based on differences in the structure of the long gonopodium of male fish. Their distribution extends from southwestern states down through Mexico as far as Colombia in the west and Guatemala and Honduras on the Atlantic (eastern) coast. None is especially well known within the aquarium hobby, although captive breeding of the gila topminnow (*P. occidentalis*) could play a vital role in safeguarding the survival of this endangered species. Its area of distribution is documented from the Gila River basin in New Mexico and Arizona, south to the coastal rivers of Sonora in Mexico, although now the surviving population is concentrated in

⬆ Green cobra guppy (*Poecilia reticulata*). One of the many ornamental forms that have been created.

◐ Small spot
topminnow
(*Poeciliopsis
paucimaculata*),
a relatively scarce
species in the
aquarium hobby,
originating from
the Río General
in Costa Rica.

➲ Barred topminnow
(*Quintana atrizona*).
The structure of the
male's gonopodium
sets these fish apart
from other
topminnows.

Bylas Spring in Arizona. Interestingly, some of the isolated populations are female only, capable of breeding without mating.

In general terms, water conditions for members of this genus can vary from soft to slightly hard, with a pH of 7 or just above, and the temperature should be about 75°F (24°C) in most cases. Superfetation is common in this group, and the young are produced over a period of time in small batches. Females may produce up to 60 fry, which are born from 28 days onward after mating.

Priapella

This genus consists of four species, the latest addition being described for the first time in 1992. Mystery surrounds *P. bonita*, however, the type specimen of which was obtained from a branch of the Río Tonto, close to the city of Refugio in the Mexican state of Veracruz. Since it was originally described in 1904, no further specimens of this species have been discovered. This has led to the suggestion that it is now extinct, with its disappearance having been linked to water pollution arising from sugar mills in the area.

Priapella spp. are powerful swimmers, with broad bodies. They are found in shallow, fast-flowing waters where there is little vegetation and where the water temperature is about 77°F (25°C). These live-bearers should therefore be kept in well-aerated surroundings. Their tank must also be kept covered at all times since the fish are capable of leaping up out of the water, often grabbing insects, which form a significant part of their natural diet. Wingless fruit-flies and gnat larvae are recommended as aquarium foods, especially as *Priapella* spp. are not keen to feed in the lower reaches of the aquarium. It may be difficult to recognize when a female is carrying young, but these fish typically produce up to about 30 fry or so, between four and eight weeks after mating. They are very social by nature, thriving in groups together.

Priapichthys

This small genus, which now consists of two species following the latest taxonomic assessment made in 1996, resembles *Brachyrhaphis* in its overall appearance (*see* page 41), although males have a longer gonopodium. The species known as *P. annectens*, originating from Costa Rica, is most widely kept, although reports suggest that the requirements of the two subspecies are significantly different. The nominate race, occurring on the eastern side of the country, is said to favor soft-water conditions with a neutral pH, whereas at least

one report suggests that *P. a. hesperis*, from the Pacific side of the country, prefers hard-water surroundings. The general consensus, however, appears to be that these livebearers are less likely to fall ill when in soft water. As to their feeding requirements, they will take both live foods and flaked food. The young, which are produced in numbers of up to 30 typically within six weeks of mating, can be reared successfully on fry foods and small invertebrates. Water quality is important for the well-being of the fry, and so good aeration and frequent partial water changes are required.

↥ Oaxacan blue eye (*Priapella intermedia*). This species takes its name from Oaxaca state in Mexico, where it is found in the Río Coatzacoalcos.

Quintana

The only member of this genus is the black-barred livebearer, also known as the barred topminnow (*Q. atrizona*), which is confined to western Cuba and the Isle of Pines. These are small fish, the more brightly colored males growing to about 1in (2.5cm) long, although the females may reach 1.6in (4cm). They can be rather nervous, so

part of their tank should be densely planted. It is better to keep them in a species-only setup, with small but regular (weekly) water changes recommended. These topminnows will take a varied diet, including small live foods. The young, numbering up to 50 in a single brood, are produced about a month after mating. They can be slow to mature, unlikely to breed until at least six months old.

Scolichthys

Only one of the two species of this Guatemalan genus is known in aquarist circles. This is the larger form, known as *S. greenwayi*. Males in this case can be up to 1.3in (3.5cm) long, while females will reach 2in (5cm). The established males in the group are often identifiable by the black edging visible on their caudal fins. They can be kept in relatively cool water, in the 68–75°F (20–24°C) range, making them most suitable for single-species aquariums. The water should be medium-hard, with a pH reading from neutral to slightly alkaline. Although live foods appear to be their favorite food, these livebearers can and should be persuaded to take a more varied diet. A typical brood consists of between 10 and 30 fry, born approximately 28 days after mating. Females can prove to be quite prolific, often producing offspring every second month.

Tomeurus

The biology of the only species in this genus, *T. gracilis*, differs significantly from virtually all other livebearers, quite simply because although internal fertilization does occur, females lay eggs rather than giving birth to live young. There is some overlap in size between the sexes, too, with males measuring 2.4–2.8in (6–7cm), whereas females grow to 2.4–3.1in (6–8cm). They are found in northern South America, ranging from Venezuela and Guyana to Suriname and Brazil, where they occur in the state of Pará. These fish have an elongated body shape, and the male's gonopodium is clearly visible. The pectoral fins are large, but perhaps the most striking feature is their big eyes. Unfortunately, *T. gracilis* is extremely rare within the aquarium hobby,

and so virtually nothing is known about its care and breeding habits, although females lay their eggs within a few days of mating.

⬆ Golden teddy (*Xenophallus umbratilis*). This is a fairly hardy aquarium occupant.

Xenodexia

Little has also been recorded about the biology of the single species, *X. ctenolepis*, which forms this genus, although it is regarded as another of the more primitive livebearers. It occurs in the Río Xalbal and Río Chixoy in El Quiche and Alta Verapaz, Guatemala, in both sluggish and fast-flowing stretches of water. These fish grow to a maximum size of about 1.6in (4cm) in the case of males and 1.8in (4.5cm) in the case of females. Once males become sexually mature, their right pectoral fin becomes modified to form a clasp that presumably helps to hold the female during mating. The gonopodium also has an unusual structure, being long and tubelike in appearance. Males will normally develop a small swordlike projection on the lower part of the caudal fin, a feature that has also been noted in some females. The water for these fish should be relatively cool, not exceeding 75°F (25°C), with a slightly hard chemical composition and an alkaline pH reading. They will eat both small live foods and dry diets. Broods are very small, and the half a dozen or so young are produced over the course of several days.

Xenophallus

This is another monotypic genus, whose sole member, *X. umbratilis*, is native to the eastern side of Costa Rica. It is considered to be a close relative of *Neoheterandria* spp. (see page 46), but males have an asymmetrical gonopodium with a pair of hornlike appendages. The male fish grows to about 2in (5cm) in length, females measure closer to 2.6in (6.5cm). Their body is elongated and streamlined, reflecting the fact that they live in fast-flowing water. These livebearers have proved to be very undemanding aquarium occupants, although partial water changes are important. A temperature of 72–79°F (22–26°C) is ideal, and they eat both live and dry foods. Females are likely to have around 25 young after a period of 28 days following mating, and broods are produced sequentially every month or so.

Xiphophorus

This large genus, comprising over 30 species, incorporates both swordtails and platies. Today, it is generally the highly ornamental aquarium strains—often created partly by hybridization—that are most widely known, rather than the individual wild strains from which these fish were derived. This is not an entirely artificial phenomenon, however, as hybridization is well documented as taking place among populations in the wild. A number of the livebearers in this group have restricted ranges, leaving them vulnerable to habitat change. Their distribution is centered in the river systems that drain into the Atlantic Ocean on the eastern side of Central America, and extends from northern Mexico south to Honduras.

The taxonomy of the different forms of *Xiphophorus* is highly contentious. The traditional view was that there were three distinctive groupings, comprising first the true swordtails, known as the Helleri group, as represented by *X. helleri*, with males displaying the characteristic swordlike projection on their caudal fin. Second was the Montezumae group, exemplified by *X. montezumae* itself, possessing only a rudimentary swordlike projection. Third, there was the Maculatus group, including fish such as the platy (*X. maculatus*), and displaying no sword.

Recent revisions to the taxonomy of these livebearers have resulted in subsequent changes to these groupings. The situation has been further complicated by discoveries of new populations of these fish. A highly distinctive form of *X. cortezi*, for example, was discovered during 1987 in the Río Talol, which flows through the Mexican state of Hidalgo. Males in this case were characterized by their large dorsal fins and by the virtual absence of a sword at the bottom of the caudal fin. Other new additions to the list include

◑ A pair of red wagtail swordtails (*Xiphophorus helleri* var.).

the species known as the sheepshead swordtail, which has been classified since 1990 as *X. birchmanni*.

The care of these livebearers is nevertheless reasonably standardized. The water chemistry should be on the alkaline side of neutral and slightly hard, and the temperature needs to be relatively low, typically 72–77°F (22–25°C). The fish can prove to be surprisingly hardy: for example, in the wild, the Montezuma swordtail (*X. montezumae montezumae*) has been recorded in water temperatures of just 58°F (14.5°C), while platies have also been found in similar environments.

FAMILY HEMIRHAMPHIDAE: HALFBEAKS

This family consists of approximately 110 species, split into around 14 genera whose distribution is centered on Southeast Asia. Members of only three of these genera are found in freshwater, although sometimes they also range into brackish waters. Others may be encountered only in a brackish environment, while marine species are included in the group as well.

Dermogenys

The members of this genus, forming part of the halfbeak family, are found widely through Southeast Asia, from Malaysia, Java, and Sumatra to Sulawesi, Borneo, and the Philippines. They occur in a range of different environments, but with the exception of the wrestling halfbeak (*D. pusillus*), they are virtually unknown in the aquarium hobby, and very little if anything is known about their habits in the wild. Some species

◑◐ Ornamental forms of the platy (*Xiphophorus maculatus* var.). A wide range of color variants now exist in this species, although red forms remain most popular.

inhabit freshwater—such as *D. montanus*, which is found in the montane forest streams close to the Bantimurung waterfalls in Sulawesi—whereas *D. pusillus* itself is often encountered in brackish areas. It is not even clear how many species should be included in this genus: the figure varies from seven to nine in total. These fish can all be identified quite easily, however, by their highly distinctive appearance, thanks to their prominent (and easily damaged) lower jaw. Their flat back and low dorsal fin reveals that they are essentially surface-dwellers, and so should have floating plants included in their aquarium for this reason.

Hemirhamphodon

The six *Hemirhamphodon* spp. are all found in freshwater, from the southern part of the Malay Peninsula south to Sumatra and west to Borneo. They require soft, acidic water conditions, and the addition of blackwater extract to their aquarium is beneficial for their well-being. The water temperature should be about 75–82°F (24–28°C). *Hemirhamphodon* halfbeaks can easily be distinguished from *Dermogenys* by the presence of teeth in their lower jaw, and by the positioning of the dorsal fin, the base of which lies in front of the anal fin. Small live foods provided on the water surface are important, but these fish may also be prepared to eat pieces of thawed live foods, although flaked food is often not favored. Males, which in this case are often larger than females, are potentially aggressive and so should be kept apart from each other. Very little has been recorded about the breeding biology of these halfbeaks, although it is known that *H. tengah* is an egg-layer. Others, such as the long-

◐ Long-snout halfbeak (*Hemirhamphodon pogonognathus*). Sexual maturity in this species is usually achieved once the fish reach just over 3in (8cm) long.

snout halfbeak (*H. pogonognathus*), are livebearing. The females of this species produce between one and four young each day, over the course of two weeks or so, with the average brood totaling about 40 fry. At this stage, the young livebearers can approach 0.8in (2cm) in length. They are born about two months after mating, and can be reared quite easily on brine shrimp nauplii.

Nomorhamphus

The taxonomy of this family has become more complex over recent years as more species have been recognized. They are attractive fish, but have a much shorter lower jaw than other halfbeaks. The protrusion is not formed by the jaw itself, but by a fleshy projection instead, which in the case of some mature males becomes black at its tip. All *Nomorhamphus* spp. occur on the island of Sulawesi (formerly known as Celebes) in Indonesia. These halfbeaks are quite brightly colored in many cases, often with brilliant red or blue markings on their fins or bodies. They are quite similar to their halfbeak relatives in their general requirements. Adequate cover is essential in the tank, as is good filtration since they inhabit stretches of clear freshwater. Up to a dozen fry may be born after a period of 60 days following mating. The young need to be separated from their parents, who are otherwise likely to prey on them, and should in turn be ready to breed when they are six months old.

Other halfbeaks

There are another 11 recognized genera of halfbeaks—including *Hyporhamphus*, *Tondanichthys*, and *Zenarchopterus*—and much still remains to be learned about the habits of this fascinating group of fish. *Hyporhamphus breederi* from South America is known to require similar water conditions to *Hemirhamphodon* spp., but other members of this genus will thrive in brackish or even marine setups. Studies involving *Hyporhamphus* suggest that they feed more readily on vegetable flaked food rather than live food, and tend to occupy the middle level in the tank. In most cases it is not known whether these halfbeaks are livebearers or egg-layers. They therefore represent interesting opportunities for study should they ever become available.

⬆ Beaufort's halfbeak (*Zenarchopterus beauforti*). This is a representative of one of the lesser known genera of halfbeaks. It is a Sri Lankan species, occurring in both brackish and fresh water, that may grow to a maximum length of 6in (15cm).

CHAPTER 3

Characteristics and Care

Livebearers rank among the easiest tropical fish to maintain in the home aquarium, particularly the widely available domesticated strains. They are often a popular choice for so-called community aquariums, which are home to a range of different species, but are equally happy when kept in groups on their own. Most livebearers, such as guppies, get on well, but male swordtails (Xiphophorus spp.) can be aggressive.

DEFINING CHARACTERISTICS

The majority of aquarium livebearers are not large fish. Sexing is normally relatively straightforward as the males can usually be identified quite easily by their smaller size compared to the females. In a number of species the males are also more brightly colored. The mouths of livebearers are upturned, indicating that they tend to seek their food in the upper reaches of the aquarium, close to or at the surface. Unlike some other groups of fish, livebearers have teeth within their mouths, which allows them to seize invertebrates and to nibble at algal growth, although there are variations reflecting the individual lifestyles of different species (see page 84).

The profile of livebearers is less easily defined, although the top of the body is often relatively flat, as is evident in the case of the

---

① IN BAD COMPANY

In order to safeguard the welfare of the livebearers in a community aquarium you need to select the other fish carefully. Things are not always straightforward in this regard. While guppies are not normally threatened by a male betta or Siamese fighting fish (*Betta splendens*), avoid selecting delta-tailed or similar guppies with elaborate fins. Otherwise, their larger companion may fatally injure the smaller fish, as it will mistake them for another of its own kind. This is especially likely if the fish are of similar coloration.

Avoid housing swordtails or more

ornamental varieties with fish such as tiger barbs (*Barbus tetrazona*) as they are notorious for their fin-nipping behavior. If you hope to rear young livebearers successfully, then it's obviously dangerous to leave them in the community aquarium, as they are likely to be preyed upon by other tank occupants, especially angelfish (*Pterophyllum* spp.) and other more predatory species. If you want to breed your fish it is also not a good idea to keep closely related species of livebearer together as the risk of hybridization would then be increased.

---

halfbeaks (Hemirhamphidae). This is another adaptation to living close to the surface. Some members of the group can even move temporarily out of the water, as in the case of the four-eyes (*Anableps* spp.). The eyes of these particular livebearers are positioned directly on top of their heads, which enables them to have a clear view above the water surface so they can spot their invertebrate prey without difficulty. The eyes of four-eyes are especially well developed, and their common name is derived from the way in which each eye is effectively partitioned into two, enabling the fish to see well both in air and under water. Part of the iris of each side of the eye is folded inward, creating two flaps that meet at the

iris

iris flap

center. The fish swims so that the water surface is at the level of this barrier. The pigmented cells at the barrier then ensure that the images received from both sides of this division are clear.

The inner structure of each of the four-eyed fish's eyes is equally remarkable. Whereas most fish can see well in water, thanks to the strong curvature of their lens, in order for the four-eye's eyes to function equally well out of water the lens needs to be flatter and therefore more convex. This difference arises from the more refractive nature of water compared with air.

While the lens serves to focus the image, the retina at the back of the eye is where the image is formed. Here again in the case of four-eyes, the retina in each eye is divided into two, with images from the water being projected onto the upper half, while those seen in the air register on the lower part. As a result, these unique and fascinating fish are able to see clearly both in air and underwater at the same time, helping them not only hunt invertebrates but also stay alert to any approaching predators. Eyes are complex enough without this extraordinary double vision!

⬆ Four-eyes (*Anableps* spp.). The eyes of these fish are specially adapted to enable them to see both in the air and underwater at the same time.

OTHER SENSORY ORGANS

On close inspection of your livebearers, you should be able to see the lateral line running down the middle of each side of the body, creating what is frequently apparent as a paler streak. This jelly-filled canal serves to detect changes in water pressure (which may indicate danger), thanks to the associated lining of nerve cells here. The nerve cells then link with the brain, allowing the fish to respond accordingly.

Livebearers are also able to hear sounds, despite the fact that sound waves do not travel well through the dense medium of water compared with air. Their ears as such are not apparent, however, and the ear chambers themselves are located behind the eyes on each side of the head. It is therefore important to avoid positioning an aquarium adjacent to a sound system of any type, as the sounds can be disturbing to the fish. The structure of the ears is also important in providing fish with their sense of balance.

The swim bladder, which serves to maintain the fish's natural buoyancy, lies in the central area of the body and is full of gas. It generally contains a higher percentage of carbon dioxide than atmospheric air. The blood vessels connecting to the air bladder facilitate gaseous exchange into and out of this organ, enabling the fish to adjust its position in the water without difficulty. Distortion of the swim bladder can occur as a developmental abnormality in some ornamental breeds of livebearers, notably balloon mollies, which are recognizable by their shortened, abnormally rotund body shape. This impairs their swimming ability. Affected individuals will have obvious difficulties in this regard, and in severe cases they will be unable to move down into deeper water.

RESPIRATION

Unlike mammals, fish do not have lungs and instead rely on their gills to extract oxygen from the water. The water is drawn in through the mouth, passing over the gills, and then exits through the operculum, a flap that covers the gills on each side of the head. As the fish exerts itself, it requires more oxygen and breathes faster; at such times the movement of the gill flaps will become more apparent.

The gill filaments within the gills have a large surface area, which makes for efficient gaseous exchange. Oxygen diffuses into the blood here, while carbon dioxide passes out of the body by the same route. A livebearer's blood is similar to ours, with red blood cells for transporting these gases around the circulatory system.

Blood is forced around the fish's body thanks to the pumping action of its heart. This is located in the vicinity of the throat, below the gills, and is divided into two chambers, the larger of which is called the atrium. The heart receives blood back from the body and then pumps it to the gills, where it is reoxygenated before being returned to the heart again and circulated through the arterial system to the body.

FIN STRUCTURES

Livebearers display the typical fin pattern associated with most fish, but the positioning and shape of their fins provides some clues as to their lifestyles. In many cases, the relatively close proximity of their dorsal and caudal fins, along with their flattened head and sleek body shape, helps them to swim quickly close to the water's surface. The dorsal fin, on the back, is naturally larger in some livebearers—notably sailfin mollies (*Poecilia latipinna*)—when its purpose is both for courtship and to intimidate would-be rivals. It also has a functional role, serving to stabilize the fish's body as it swims forward, while if the rear part is curled it can slow the fish's swimming speed. Main propulsion comes from the caudal (tail) fin; pronounced forking here indicates a fast-swimming species.

The maneuverability of livebearers in the water is further aided by the pectoral fins, which are located relatively high up on each side of the body and act as brakes when necessary. The pelvic fins are positioned farther forward in livebearers than in a number of

⬆ Balloon mollies are recognizable by their rotund and rather compacted body shape, which can result in distortion of the swim bladder.

The length of the gonopodium can give an insight into the lifestyle of a particular species. Male pike minnows (*Belonesox belizanus*), for example, have a long gonopodium, which means that they do not have to approach as close to their larger female partner as guppies (*Poecilia reticulata*) when mating. This helps to ensure that if a female is not ready to mate, the male pike minnow can dart away from potential danger more easily, rather than ending up as her next meal.

other groups of fish, helping to keep them on a level trajectory in the water. In the case of members of the subfamily Anablepinae, the strength of these side fins is such that they even allow these livebearers to haul themselves out of the water.

THE COPULATORY ORGAN

The most distinctive feature of the fin structure of this group of fish is the way in which the male's anal fin has been modified to form a copulatory organ, known as a gonopodium. This allows sperm to be channeled directly into the female's body during mating, rather than simply being released randomly into the water, as occurs with egg-laying fish. Gonopodiums are of various lengths, depending upon the species concerned, and can measure up to 1in (2.5cm). The gonopodium consists of a series of rays, which are the supporting central areas of the fins. Yet under the microscope, the arrangement of these rays—notably from the third to the fifth—differs quite widely, and so this characteristic feature can be used to determine relationships within the group.

Variations on the theme

The structure of the gonopodium varies significantly throughout this group of fish. It is at its most primitive in the case of the goodeids, and their arrangement may give some insight into how the organ developed. Close study of the anal fin in this case merely reveals a

◐ Viscera of male swordtail (*Xiphophorus helleri*).

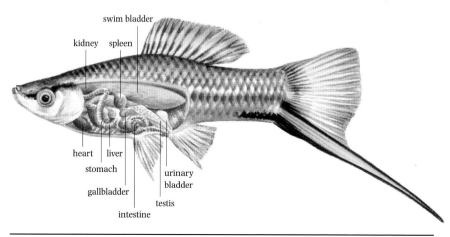

swim bladder

kidney spleen

heart | liver
stomach
gallbladder
intestine
urinary bladder
testis

narrowing of the space separating the first five or seven rays, which are also shortened in length. This results in the formation of a notch at the front part of the fin, called a spermatopodium, which allows sperm to be ejaculated into the female's body during mating. In order for this arrangement to work successfully, the goodeids engage in more pronounced courtship rituals, since the likelihood of mating failure can be higher as contact time between the fish has to be longer.

The anal fin structure of male anablepids differs markedly from that of the goodeids, being tubelike in appearance. This enables sperm to flow, in contrast to the more open arrangement associated with guppies and related species. The rays at the tip of the gonopodium are actually twisted around themselves, resulting in a structure that bears some resemblance to a penis. (Though the organ does not really function like a mammalian penis.)

A different and distinctive arrangement is associated with members of the halfbeak family, Hemirhamphidae, to the extent that the male organ in this case is often described as an andropodium. There is a kneelike bend known as the geniculus apparent on the second ray of their anal fin, approximately halfway down its length, with a pair of associated spines known as the tridens flexilis at its tip. The skin separating the third and fourth rays also creates a distinctive pouch, which is described as the physa.

HORMONAL INFLUENCES

The change in the structure of the anal fin of livebearers is controlled by hormones, as has been demonstrated by some unscrupulous breeders. Administering the so-called "male" hormone, in the form of a testosterone derivative, to female swordtails (*Xiphophorus helleri*) will not only cause the development of apparent "male" fish, but also results in the development of a gonopodium, although such fish will prove to be infertile.

ⓘ MATING PROBLEMS

In some fancy varieties, such as the lyretailed form of the swordtail (*Xiphophorus helleri*), the gonopodium has become much longer and more distorted than normal so that these particular males cannot mate successfully under normal circumstances. Female lyretails in this case must be paired with the males of other varieties, the resulting offspring then should consist of both lyretailed and normal-tailed fish in roughly equal numbers, accordng to the laws of genetics. On occasions, lyretailed males have been used to sire others by means of artificial insemination. This technique has also been used in other cases when the gonopodium has been damaged and lacks the so-called "holdfast mechanism" normally present at the tip of this modified fin, thereby rendering the fish unable to mate.

These apparent differences in the structure of the copulatory organ of male livebearers are critical to their continued reproductive success. They serve to lessen the likelihood of hybridization occurring in the wild, where different species are often found in the same waters. Variations occur not just in the length of the organ but also at its tip to help ensure that random matings are unlikely to be successful, except between closely related species. This applies even more in those livebearers with gonopodiums deviated either to the right- or left-hand side of the body, as this development precludes males mating with all the females in the population. Such species can breed successfully only with females that have a corresponding genital opening. (This throws down an interesting challenge to the definition of species as closely related animals that can breed!)

Fin variants

Changes in fin structure in a number of different species of livebearer are now well established. These include hi-fin stock, where the dorsal fin is significantly larger. This change first arose in swordtails, and was then transferred to platy lines by subsequent hybridization. The hi-fin feature has proved to be genetically dominant, so that using a single hi-fin as a parent should result in fish of similar appearance being present within each brood. This is not to say that their dorsal fins are a consistent size or shape, and a fairly common fault is that some of the individual rays forming the fin are deviated backward. This flaw is often referred to by breeders as a "pinched dorsal."

These particular members of the poeciliid group are naturally susceptible to variations in the shape of their fins, as shown by the fact that lyretailed variants have been recorded not just in swordtails, but also in guppies and mollies. Some wild individuals display a tendency to modifications of this type, a feature that has subsequently been developed by selective breeding. In the case of the guppy (*Poecilia reticulata*), there are approximately 12 common variants in terms of fin type.

The lyretailed form was the first to be created, back in the early 1950s. These fish can now be grouped into various subcategories, based on their appearance. The triangular or delta-tailed form, for example, is a more extreme version of the fantailed, in which the caudal fin is of a larger size.

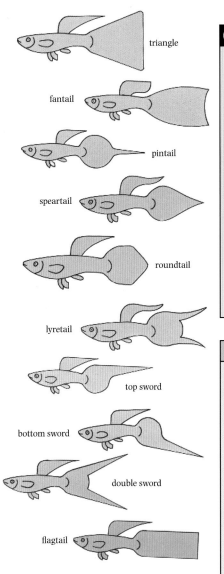

❶ Variations associated with the dorsal and caudal fins of guppies (*Poecilia reticulata*) are portrayed here. These have been evolved through selective breeding, allowing distinctive strains of such fish to be developed, irrespective of their coloration and markings.

ⓘ NOT A HELP!

The increased surface area of the caudal fin, which is most marked in delta-tailed guppies, does not necessarily improve the swimming ability of such fish. In some instances, particularly if the fin droops in the water, the guppy may even encounter more difficulty than normal in swimming. The fact that such change does not reflect a survival advantage for these fish in the wild is further reflected by the finding that all wild guppy populations are comprised of small-finned males. None has been recorded as displaying an increase in the size of its fins in the manner of the domesticated cousins.

ACRYLIC AQUARIUMS

Aquariums made of acrylic do have the advantage of being significantly lighter in weight than their glass counterparts, although their surface can be scratched quite easily. Not only is this often unsightly, but scratches on the inside of the tank are then easily colonized by algae, which will be almost impossible to remove and will create green streaks as a result. When washing out an acrylic tank, avoid using very hot water as this can potentially cloud the surface and may also distort the lid. Acrylic tanks can break easily when dropped, as with glass, so they need to be handled with equal care, particularly if they are wet on the outside.

HOUSING OPTIONS

One of the advantages as an aquarist of choosing livebearers is that most species are relatively small. A group of guppies (*Poecilia reticulata*), for example, can therefore be housed and bred successfully in one of the relatively small complete kit tanks designed with all the necessary components in place. These are made of molded acrylic, although glass tanks are equally satisfactory.

The development of aquarium sealant led to the creation of so-called frameless tanks, by allowing sheets of glass to be stuck firmly together. While this sealant forms a watertight bond, it does not dry out completely but seals with significant force to absorb the water pressure when the aquarium is full. Only in bigger tanks exceeding 24in (60cm) in length are supporting horizontal crossbars required. It is worthwhile checking that a new tank is watertight when washing it out, and it is also recommended that you remove any dirt or spicules of glass that might be present. A visual check prior to purchase can be useful, just to ensure the sealant is evenly distributed around the joins between the sheets of glass. There is a slight risk that there may be a small area where the bonding is not complete, and this will result in a leak. Some glass aquariums are fitted with a plastic surround, which gives protection to the more vulnerable points. If not, take particular care to avoid resting an all-glass aquarium on its corners as these units are easily damaged here—any resulting chipping of the glass can seriously weaken the tank.

POSITIONING THE AQUARIUM

Avoid drafty areas such as hallways, or rooms where the temperature fluctuates markedly over the course of a day. Within a room, certain localities can also have undesirable effects on the water temperature. Never position an aquarium next to a radiator for this reason, or in a window bay where the sun's rays can easily cause overheating, as this can have potentially fatal consequences. Bright lighting is also likely to lead to an unwanted excess of algal growth, affecting not just the sides but also the décor, and possibly choking the plants as well. In many cases, you will need to invest in a suitable stand for the aquarium, although you may already have a suitable table or something similar that can be used. Position the tank at a comfortable height so that you can see the fish when sitting down and relaxing, and can attend to their needs easily. A location close to a power point is helpful, so that you do not need to trail electrical wires around the room.

If you have space in your home, you may prefer to invest in a cabinet for your aquarium. These are available in a variety of styles, and incorporate space for external electrical equipment and filters. Such units are significantly more costly than a basic stand, but are particularly ideal for accommodating some of the less typical aquarium designs that are now available—those that are triangular in shape can be fitted into the corner of a room.

Whether you choose a stand or cabinet, however, be sure to check that the unit is exactly horizontal. If it is tilting for any reason, it will not only look unattractive but the unevenness may place additional stress on the tank. You probably need a secure wedge to prop up the feet at the lower end of the stand. As a further precaution, it is strongly recommended that all-glass tanks rest on a styrofoam sheet cut to the size of the base.

PLAN AHEAD

It is vital to be sure that the aquarium is correctly positioned before you start to fill it. Even a small tank is almost impossible to move without being emptied first, as each gallon of water weighs 8lb (each liter weighs 1kg) and the capacity of a typical aquarium is in excess of 8 gallons (30 liters). The size of the tank you choose depends on a number of factors, not just the space you have available. A large aquarium is obviously more costly, not only to set up but also to maintain in terms of heating and lighting costs, although it offers more scope for you to enjoy the fish. Since livebearers generally reproduce readily, it can be advantageous to have extra space available in the aquarium for the young fish produced. A

⬆ The positioning of the aquarium can directly affect the health of the occupants. These are red swordtails (*Xiphophorus helleri*). They require a relatively large, well aerated aquarium.

larger tank also allows you to add fish of different species that are compatible with the livebearers as far as water chemistry and behavior go. Guppies and other common livebearers are often housed with various smaller barbs and tetras, for example, both of which live in schools, as well as some smaller catfish. Corydoras catfish are a popular choice as they spend most of their time on or near the substrate, and so will not interfere with the livebearers.

HOW MANY FISH?

Working out the potential stocking density of an aquarium is straightforward, and is based on the tank's surface area. This figure is critical to the well-being of the fish, because the surface is where oxygen diffuses into the water and carbon dioxide comes out of solution. To calculate the surface area, multiply the length of the tank by its width in inches (or centimeters). It is usually recommended to allow about 12sq in (77sq cm) for each inch (2.5cm) of livebearer, excluding the length of its tail. Avoid stocking the aquarium to its maximum at the outset, not just because the fish are likely to grow in size, but also because the filtration system takes time to become fully effective.

FILTRATION SYSTEMS

Undergravel filters

An undergravel filter is the type most common in aquariums housing livebearers. As its name suggests, such a filter needs to be placed directly on the floor of the aquarium, with the gravel then being

◑ Festival platy (*Xiphophorus maculatus* var.). Effective filtration helps to ensure that fish will remain healthy.

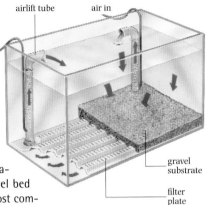

airlift tube   air in

gravel
substrate

filter
plate

tipped on top. Undergravel filters are very simple, consisting of what is effectively a corrugated sheet across which holes are evenly distributed. These filters are manufactured in various sizes corresponding to the tanks themselves, and it is important that the plate fits right across the entire base of the aquarium. This means that for tanks of unusual shapes, the filter may have to be cut with a craft knife or similar tool.

There are two methods of undergravel filtration, both of which rely on an adequate gravel bed that must be at least 3in (7.5cm) deep. The most commonly used system sees water flowing down through the gravel, although in reverse filtration the water passes upward through the filter. In either case, relatively coarse gravel should be chosen to ensure the effectiveness of the filter. If the gravel is too fine, with a consistency approaching sand, it blocks the pores of the filter and hence the development of beneficial bacteria is restricted.

The airlift tube slots onto a corner of the filter plate at the back of the aquarium, where it can be disguised more easily. The other piece of equipment that is necessary is the air pump, which drives the system and is located outside the aquarium. The connecting tubing must be fitted with a non-return valve to prevent water running back into the pump.

The purpose of the air pump is to assist in drawing the water through the filter bed, which operates on the basis of a process known as biological filtration. The pump helps to seed the tank with a beneficial bacterial culture that speeds up the development of the filter at the outset.

The bacteria in the system, which require oxygen and are therefore aerobic, ultimately break down the fishes' waste and play a key part in the nitrogen cycle. They are responsible for converting toxic ammonia first to nitrite and then to nitrate, which is finally extracted from the water as a fertilizer by the plants growing in the tank. It takes about eight weeks for this type of filter to start working at maximum efficiency, and subsequently it needs little maintenance. The gravel should be sloped from the back of the tank down to the front, so that any mulm (solid waste) is visible and can be siphoned out. It is also a good idea to use a gravel cleaner every two weeks or so when carrying out a partial water change in the aquarium, so that the gravel bed does not become blocked by dirt. Otherwise this buildup restricts the flow of the water, and the resulting lack of oxygen then reduces the efficiency of the system.

◐ A conventional-flow undergravel filter system. Water is drawn down through the filter bed (substrate) and returned via the airlift tube back to the top of the aquarium.

Power filters

There is now a range of other types of filter systems available, of which power filters are especially popular, although because of their design these need to be used carefully in aquariums containing young fish (the fry can be sucked into the filter). At its most basic, a power filter comprises a motor and a filter sponge. Water is drawn in through slits at the base of the unit, passing through the sponge before being returned to the aquarium via the outflow at the top of the unit. This type of filter provides not only biological filtration, with the establishment of a bacterial population on the filter itself, but also mechanical filtration, where larger particles in the water become enmeshed in the sponge and remain trapped. Other, more sophisticated power filters contain different types of media. These are more suitable for larger aquariums. They often contain charcoal, which provides a third type of filtration, known as chemical filtration. This is useful for removing toxic substances from the water, but should not be used in tanks containing medication, as it renders it useless.

When deciding on a power filter, it is important to choose one that is suitable for your size of aquarium. Internal power filters, which can be incorporated inside the tank, are suitable for smaller aquariums, but for larger setups an external power filter is recommended. This can then be concealed outside the aquarium. Again, remember that this type of filter is not suitable for breeding setups as the fry can be sucked in—always check the inflow when choosing a model to minimize this danger. The components of a power filter need to be serviced, which is best done when carrying out a partial water change. You can then rinse the sponge off in the bucket of tank water before this is discarded (avoid rinsing it in fresh tapwater as this will kill off the beneficial bacteria established here).

As they create a noticeable current, power filters are most useful in aquariums housing livebearers that naturally occur in fast-flowing waters, such as knifefish (*Alfaro* spp.). More gentle sponge filters, which are comprised of a piece of foam through which water passes, are a safe option for both fry and those fish from tranquil surroundings.

HEATING CONTROL

Most aquariums today are heated by means of a single combined heater unit rather than a separate heater and thermostat. Heaters are

---

① BRACKISH WATER WARNING

The application of the chemical zeolite to a newly established aquarium can be useful in helping to remove toxic ammonia before it can cause any harm to the fish. It comes in the form of a packet, but it is not of any real value in a brackish-water aquarium setup, simply because the salt in the water prevents the zeolite from functioning effectively.

---

available in various wattages, the more powerful being required in larger aquariums. The size of the unit may also be significant in the case of smaller setups, where more compact designs are obviously better. Most heaters are now supplied preset to about 75°F (24°C), but check how easily the figure can be adjusted if required. On safety grounds, it is better to buy a unit that switches off automatically if it is accidentally lifted out of the water while still in operation. The length of the models varies, with the shorter designs obviously preferable for smaller, shallow-water setups. As a general guide, allow about 2 watts per gallon (3.8 liters) of water—a small, 10 gallon (38-liter) tank therefore requires a 20 watt heater.

All-in-one aquarium units incorporate an area for the heater in their design, concealing it so that it cannot be seen. In other cases, you need to stick the heater onto the side of the tank so that the heater component is located near the base of the aquarium. It needs to be in a reasonably open stretch of water so that there is no possibility that localized and potentially dangerous heat spots will develop in the tank.

You can monitor the temperature within the aquarium easily, by means of an LCD thermometer stuck onto the outside of the tank at the front. An alternative is to use a traditional alcohol-filled aquarium thermometer, which should be stuck on the inside of the glass directly in the water. These do, however, require reading with closer scrutiny.

○ A range of aquarium equipment.
1 Heaters that incorporate thermostats alongside the heater.
2 An external thermostat with a temperature probe.
3 A standard alcohol thermometer alongside a combined hydrometer and thermometer, plus a digital strip thermometer.
4 A liquid crystal display (LCD) thermometer.

In areas where heating requirements are minimal, or when you simply want to cool the fishes' quarters for a period of time (as with some goodeids), consider a heating pad as an alternative to a heater. Again, these are available in various dimensions corresponding to the size of individual aquariums. They are usually fitted out of sight, directly beneath the aquarium, although they can also be stuck directly onto the side so that they emit gentle heat through the glass or through an acrylic panel. A remote thermostat placed in the tank regulates the heat output from such pads.

LIGHTING

Aquariums housing livebearers need good illumination, and not just in order to allow you to see the fish—it also leads to the growth of green algae, which supplements the fishes' diet. Fluorescent tubes designed for aquarium hoods mimic the effect of natural sunlight, and are available in various lengths to suit all standard sizes. The hood needs to fit snugly over the tank, partly to prevent evaporation of the water and also to minimize the risk of external contamination of the water. Guidance regarding the correct lighting system for a particular aquarium really depends on the lights themselves: check the packaging to be sure you make the right choice.

Care must be taken to ensure that the lighting electrics are not allowed to come into direct contact with any water, although the connections are well protected in most modern designs of tank hood. To prevent the aquarium from becoming overgrown with algae, you need to experiment at first in order to determine how long the lights should be left on each day. The algae can grow to such an extent that it ultimately kills plants growing in the tank, nevertheless there must be sufficient light of the correct wavelength to ensure the growth of the aquarium plants or they will simply die off. Plants require sunlight (or a suitable substitute) to provide them with the necessary source of energy so they can photosynthesize and grow. The actual light output from the sunlight tubes is quite low, however, and this may need to be combined with a brighter tube so that the occupants of the aquarium are illuminated. In most aquariums, leaving the light on for 10–12 hours per day should be sufficient to attain the correct balance.

⚠ ORDINARY LIGHTBULBS

Incandescent lights are not recommended for aquarium use, partly because they do not produce light from the right part of the spectrum to encourage plant growth. They also emit a considerable amount of heat, which may affect the temperature of the water itself.

AQUARIUM GRAVEL

The substrate of the tank is an important consideration, not only in aesthetic terms but also because it can affect the water chemistry

in the aquarium. Limestone-based gravel will dissolve gradually over a period of time, making the water harder. An increasing range of different types of gravel is now available for use as the floor covering in a tank. These gravels may be colored or just white, but bear in mind when choosing the former that the more garish shades can easily detract from the appearance of the fish. As an example, orange swordtails (*Xiphophorus helleri*) appear quite dull when swimming above red gravel, while white gravel may make an attractive contrast in a tank housing black mollies (*Poecilia sphenops* var.). In the case of dyed gravel, it is important that the color remains fast and will not leach out. Plasticized gravel affords another alternative, and is available in a similar mix of colors. When it comes to deciding how much gravel you need for a tank, allow about 3lb (1kg) per 1.6 gallons (4.5 liters) of water in order to provide an adequate covering.

Aquarium gravel is usually sold in a prewashed form in bags, but it is not a good idea simply to tip this into the aquarium. Although this gravel may appear reasonably clean, the likelihood is that it contains fine particles of sand—once you fill up the aquarium with water, a scum will form on the surface and the main body will be cloudy. This can be a difficult problem to overcome and will detract significantly from the finished appearance of the setup, so it is worthwhile washing the gravel first under a running faucet. A colander is ideal for this task, along with a clean bucket.

Start by tipping the gravel into the bucket, and then add a special aquarium disinfectant to kill off any harmful organisms. Leave the gravel in this solution for a few hours, stirring it occasionally, before tipping it out in small batches into the colander and rinsing it very thoroughly. Once you are certain that the gravel is clean, pour it carefully into the tank on top of the undergravel filter. This is now the stage at which you can add the heater and other décor within the tank.

❶ Careful planning is important to create an attractive aquarium. Mapping out the position of rockwork and plants beforehand on paper is sensible. Wash gravel before putting it into the tank.

⊕ Mexican oak-leaf plant (*Shinnersia rivularis*). If set in a group, these plants provide a valuable retreat for young livebearers.

PLANTING SCHEMES

While the aim of a planting scheme is obviously to make the aquarium look attractive, its design should be based primarily on the needs of the fish, so that they are living in as natural an environment as possible. There are differences in this respect between the various livebearers. For example, those guppies (*Poecilia reticulata*) with elaborate tailfins, such as delta-tails, benefit from having relatively clear areas of water so that they can swim easily. Predatory pike minnows (*Belonesox belizanus*), which naturally lurk in dense aquatic vegetation to ambush passing prey, benefit not just from the presence of plants, but also from carefully constructed rockwork retreats where they can hide. Some livebearers such as halfbeaks (Hemirhamphidae) even prove nervous if housed in a tank that affords them little seclusion. In this case it is not only a matter of adding plants to the body of the water itself, but also floating plants to provide cover at the water's surface, where these fish spend much of their time.

Bear in mind that you will need to be able to see the fish, so you should incorporate a clear area at the front of the aquarium. A typical plan for a tank includes a specimen plant, which can grow into a focal point in the center toward the back, plus some denser planting around the periphery. Plants on rocks and woodwork should also be included, as should floating plants on the surface.

CHOOSING AQUARIUM PLANTS

A wide range of aquarium plants is available, but your choice will be influenced by the water conditions the fish themselves require. It is also important to choose plants that correspond to the layout and size of the tank. Relatively dense, low-level cover can be important in a tank housing livebearers as it provides a suitable retreat where fry can seek refuge.

Since many livebearers are housed in quite small aquariums, it is important to select only those plants that will not outgrow the tank. The ruffled Amazon sword (*Echinodorus major*), for example, may grow leaves 20in (50cm) long; a better option in a livebearer setup may be the pygmy chain swordplant (*E. tenellus*), which grows typically to about 6in (15cm) in comparison. Local aquatic stores usually stock a range of the more adaptable and easily grown plants. However, if you want a larger choice you may have to seek out one of the mail-order aquatic plant nurseries, which usually advertise in the fish keeping magazines or can be located through the Internet.

Most aquatic plants grow well within the temperature range of a typical aquarium for livebearers, although they often tend to favor the upper end of that range. There are hardy examples that occur within the natural distribution of some of these fish, such as the tropical water violet (*Hottonia inflata*), which originates from the southeastern U.S. It is an adaptable plant, too, with regards its water chemistry needs. Another useful plant in this respect is the Mexican oak-leaf plant (*Shinnersia rivularis*), which is typically incorporated toward the rear of the aquarium. It can be grown easily from cuttings or by splitting off runners.

Since the roots of many aquarium plants spread readily through the substrate, they may invade the slits in the undergravel filter, blocking them off. It is often better to restrict the growth of plants by setting them in small plastic pots, which can be buried in the substrate and concealed by rocks or woodwork. There is a significant difference between typical land plants and those that live in water, in that the roots of the latter primarily serve to provide anchorage rather than as a major conduit for nutrients. Nevertheless, if conditions are unfavorable then the plants will not thrive. You should always expect some dieback after moving plants into a new aquarium, but you can reduce this by ensuring that the leaves are not left to dry out and by transferring the plants back to water as soon as possible.

Before positioning plants, ensure that they are not contaminated with aquatic snails. In a well-established aquarium a few snails will not cause serious damage, but a group can decimate newly established plants. Their eggs appear as blobs of jelly, stuck on the underside of the leaves—breaking off affected leaves is the easiest way of dealing with them. You may also want to dip the plants in a solution of aquarium disinfectant to kill off harmful microbes.

It is easier to put the plants in place once the aquarium is about half-full of water, as they are then less likely to be displaced when the tank is topped up. Floating plants should only be put in once the aquarium is completed, or they will get in the way. To minimize the stress on the plants when you introduce them, check that the water itself is near the correct temperature. You may find it helpful to use a planting stick if you have odd cuttings to set in place. Start at the back of the

● The choice of aquarium backdrop has a great impact.

● Pygmy chain sword (*Echinodorus tenellus*). Vegetation will soften the appearance of rockwork in the aquarium.

aquarium and work forward round the sides so that you can plan the design, carrying out any necessary adjustments as you go. Try to avoid positioning plants directly adjacent to the heater, as they are unlikely to thrive in such close proximity to this unit, although that said they can often be used in such a way as to conceal its presence.

PLANTING CONSIDERATIONS

Not all aquatic plants used in the aquarium are grown from cuttings. Some, notably relatives of the hardy waterlilies, grow from tubers. A number of these are popular as the centerpiece of a tank, for both their growth and the color of their leaves. The red form of the African tiger lotus (*Nymphaea maculata*) has large, rounded, and attractively blotched reddish leaves, with purple undersides. It requires bright lighting conditions to thrive, but is reasonably adaptable with regards its water chemistry needs, and will even flower in the aquarium.

The way in which water plants are set in the substrate is crucial to their well-being, as if they are planted too deeply, with their growing shoots covered by gravel, they often simply rot away. Always leave the growing shoot exposed above the surface of the gravel for this reason, rather than burying it.

In the early stages after setting up the aquarium, there is a possibility that the livebearers will start nibbling at the plants. This situation is made worse because at this time there is an absence of algae, which features prominently in the diet of species such as mollies. As the aquarium settles down, the fish not only start feeding on the algae that develops, but the growth of the plants is sufficiently vigorous to withstand the attention of the fish themselves.

The situation is likely to be worsened if you introduce aquatic snails alongside the fish, particularly in these early stages, as they too will feed on the vegetation. Worse still, mature snails lay hundreds of eggs, and the aquarium becomes overrun by these invertebrates. It is therefore important to curb their numbers by removing the eggs as they are laid. They are produced in a jellylike casing, which may be deposited anywhere around the aquarium, usually on the plants or on the glass itself.

During the early stages, there is less beneficial nitrate in solution from the breakdown of the fishes' waste, as biological filtration will take several weeks to develop effectively. It may therefore be particularly helpful to the plants at this stage if you add a special aquarium fertilizer. A more traditional alternative is to bury a rabbit dropping close to the roots in the gravel.

Initial dieback of plants introduced to the aquarium is most likely in the case of those with elaborate leaves. This is far less likely to be encountered with floating plants, which simply have to be dropped onto the surface of the aquarium, although if you have a power filter the currents will sweep them to a particular part of the tank. This means that you may need to adjust the outflow to ensure that the plants are directed to a suitable area.

Floating plants are ideal for livebearers that naturally occupy relatively shallow waters, providing them with cover, but there must be adequate space between the top of the tank and the surface of the water. Otherwise, the plants are liable to dampen off, turning moldy thanks to water dripping down on them from the hood. Under favorable conditions, members of this group of plants spread quite rapidly, pieces may have to be removed from the tank to curtail their growth. This is necessary to allow adequate light to reach plants in the lower reaches of the aquarium, as well as to encourage algal growth. Some livebearers nibble floating plants to supplement their diet, but the robust growth of these plants makes them less likely to be affected than those set in the substrate.

ROCKS AND WOODWORK

When you choose rockwork, it may be better to avoid limestone as this will dissolve into the water over a period of time, increasing its hardness as a result. Inert rocks such as granite are a better choice, particularly for livebearers that are naturally occuring in softwater

◑ Rockwork is heavy and needs to be firmly positioned within the aquarium. Consider using a variety of rocks with different colors, as here.

areas. Suitable rockwork is available from aquatic outlets. Choose shapes that appeal to you and that don't look out of place in the aquarium. It is important not to incorporate too much rockwork, because this can reduce the efficiency of the undergravel filter by restricting the movement of water through the substrate.

Clean the rockwork thoroughly before adding it to the aquarium, scrubbing it with a brush in a solution of aquarium disinfectant and then rinsing it off carefully. It is worth bearing in mind that all rockwork is relatively heavy, and so should not be piled up randomly within the tank as it may cause it to collapse. If you want to fix two pieces of rockwork together, use aquarium sealant for the purpose. There are also lightweight rock substitutes available, which may be safer to use in some circumstances.

Special bogwood suitable for the aquarium can be obtained easily from most aquatic outlets, and as with rockwork it can provide valuable retreats for livebearers while adding to the visual appeal of the aquarium. Always soak bogwood in a bucket for several days before use, changing the water frequently. This reduces the amount of tannin that can leach out from the wood into the water, which would turn it yellow. Alternatively, the wood can be varnished and left to dry thoroughly, thereby sealing the tannin into the wood, although there are some fears about toxicity with this method. These concerns have led to the development of some quite realistic bogwood substitutes.

Both rockwork and bogwood offer the potential to create a more appealing underwater scene since there are plants that can be

JAVA MOSS

This plant is native to Southeast Asia, but has proved to be very adaptable and thrives even under conditions of subdued lighting. It appears quite a dark shade of green in this case, becoming lighter when the level of illumination is higher. Java moss is easy to propagate, and if you buy a clump you can simply split it and wrap the divisions individually around pieces of bogwood and rocks, securing them with rubber bands. It soon becomes established in these new surroundings, anchoring itself firmly in place. You can then cut the bands off, and the new fronds will rapidly grow to provide an ideal retreat for young fish. Used carefully, Java moss also helps to soften the appearance of what can otherwise be a rather bare setup.

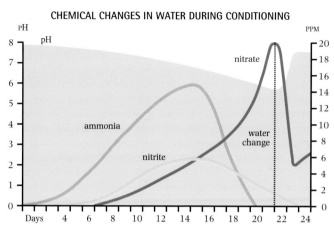

CHEMICAL CHANGES IN WATER DURING CONDITIONING

pH

PPM

ammonia

nitrite

nitrate

water change

Days 4 6 8 10 12 14 16 18 20 22 24

● What happens typically to nitrate, nitrite, and ammonia levels during conditioning when the water is not changed. In an established aquarium, ammonia and nitrites should be close to undetectable. The nitrate levels are normal, so the biological filtration system is operating. As soon as the water is changed, nitrate levels plummet and pH is readjusted.

grown on these types of surfaces. Once established, such plants also provide an important refuge for young livebearers—Java moss (*Vesicularia dubyana*) is especially valued in this regard (see box).

Another similarly adaptable plant that grows well when the lighting conditions may be less than ideal is Java fern (*Microsorium pteropus*). Grow this plant in a similar way to Java moss, attaching it to the décor in the aquarium rather than setting it in the gravel. A dense clump again provides lifesaving cover for fry until they are large enough to avoid being preyed upon by other fish. Strands of Java fern grow to at least 10in (25cm), so that in a relatively shallow aquarium its growth may extend above the water's surface, where its appearance is transformed. This adds to its appeal in such surroundings, as the plant is able to colonize an area that can otherwise be hard to decorate successfully. Tank backdrops, which fit onto the rear of the aquarium, obviously look out of place when part of the display is above the water level.

WATER CHEMISTRY

The chemical composition of water varies in some crucial respects from area to area, depending on where it has originated. Water taken from rivers is likely to have very different chemical properties to that which has been filtered through chalk and drawn from aquifers. The relative hardness of a sample of water is influenced by the proportion of dissolved salts it contains. There are two distinct types of hardness: temporary hardness, resulting from the presence of carbonate ions, which can be removed by boiling; and permanent hardness, caused by sulfates. The relative hardness of a sample of water also has an impact on the degree of acidity, or pH, of the sample. This is measured on a logarithmic scale, which means that even a small change can be significant. Readings below pH7 (which is neutral) are defined as acidic, whereas those above this figure are alkaline. Most livebearers occur in waters that are hard and therefore have a pH on the alkaline side of neutral. Those found in Jalisco, Mexico, for example, inhabit waters that have flowed over limestone and are hard and alkaline. Within the same area there are those found in slow flowing streams containing a high degree of humus, created from dead leaves and other vegetation, and this results in more acidic conditions.

Most domesticated livebearers are relatively adaptable in terms of their water chemistry requirements, having often been bred under water conditions that differ from those found in their native habitats. Stock of wild origins is likely to be much more dependent on a water chemistry that approximates that of their natural habitat. If such conditions are not met, this does not necessarily mean that the fish will become ill, but it does mean that they are more likely to succumb to minor infections, may be less brightly colored than normal, and may fail to breed well.

Water test kits

It is simple to monitor water chemistry by means of test kits marketed for aquarium use. These are sold in the form of reagents, which need to be mixed with a sample of tank water. They are supplied typically with a color chart that enables the result to be read off. Alternatively, a selection of LCD display meters are available, which enable readings to be taken immediately simply by inserting the probe into the aquarium water, although these are more expensive than the simple test kits.

You need to check the water regularly, not just at the outset, because changes will occur in the chemistry in the aquarium over a period of time. What happens is that bicarbonates and carbonates present in the water combine with hydrogen, serving to stabilize the pH. Once this so-called buffering system is used up, however, the water becomes both softer and acidic, forming conditions that are less favorable to the majority of

---

MEASUREMENT OF WATER HARDNESS

Water hardness can be measured on several different scales, although today it is usually quoted in mg/liter, and sometimes as degrees of general hardness (dGH). The following table indicates the typical divisions:

mg/l	dGH	Description
0–50	0–5	very soft
50–100	6–9 dGH	soft–moderately soft
100–150	10–14 dGH	slightly–medium hard
150–200	15–19 dGH	moderately hard
200–300	20–28 dGH	hard
over 300	over 28 dGH	very hard

Water quality checks can be carried out using special test kits, with the results being easily assessed on the basis of the accompanying color charts.

livebearers. The changes can be offset to some extent by placing calcium-containing rockwork in the aquarium. Such rocks dissolve over a period of time, acting as a further source of carbonate. The best solution, however, is to carry out regular partial water changes, replacing approximately a quarter of the water in the aquarium with fresh water that has been treated with a conditioner. This also helps to dilute other potentially harmful chemicals that may otherwise accumulate in the water, including nitrates.

Other chemical additives

Domestic water supplies are likely to contain either chlorine or chloramine, which is added to it as a disinfectant. Unfortunately, such chemicals are toxic to fish, even at very dilute concentrations. In most cases, chlorine dissipates from the water if it has been left to stand for a day or two, but chloramine can remain in solution for a week. It is therefore very important to add a suitable dechlorinator to neutralize such chemicals, both before introducing the fish and when carrying out a water change.

Water conditioners are added in the required volume to the water in the tank. They often incorporate other additives, such as aloe vera, which helps to prevent skin damage. This problem can sometimes arise if the protective coating of mucus on the fish's body is damaged when the fish is caught or handled. Always try to avoid handling a fish directly, but if you do need to pick one up, ensure that your hands are wet as this causes less damage.

Achieving the correct salinity

Some livebearers naturally inhabit brackish waters, and certain members of the group, such as mollies, are often maintained in this type of environment and remain healthier as a result. In such cases

◯ Threadjaw halfbeak (*Hemirhamphodon pogonognathus*). This is one of the livebearers found in brackish water.

it is necessary to replicate these conditions in your aquarium, and this can be done by adding to the water a carefully formulated salt mixture, as sold primarily for marine fish keeping. A weak solution should be made up following the instructions on the packaging. Never be tempted to use table salt for this purpose.

The level of salinity in the water is measured by its specific gravity (SG) reading. The SG of pure freshwater is 1.000, whereas the sea is likely to have an SG measurement of about 1.020. Brackish water conditions fall between these two figures, and as far as livebearers are concerned, an SG not exceeding 1.010 is suitable.

When preparing a brackish environment, you need to add the marine salt in the right quantity to a bucket of water, stirring this thoroughly with a wooden spoon to dissolve it. Only a small quantity of salt is needed, typically the equivalent of 5ml (a teaspoonful) per gallon (4.5 liters), although this can be increased to 7.5ml (1½ teaspoons) in the case of halfbeaks (Hemirhamphidae).

The decor is influenced by the salt in the water, especially with regard to the choice of plants, as not all species will grow well under these conditions (see box). You may decide instead to opt for plastic plants—very realistic natural substitutes are available today. These are essentially maintenance-free, although they may need occasional cleaning if their leaves become covered with algae. There are drawbacks to using artificial plants, whether in freshwater or brackish surroundings, because they do not remove dissolved nitrates from the water as happens when living plants are present.

A side effect of this is that algal growth within the aquarium is likely to be more prominent, simply because the algae utilize the nitrates (that serve as a fertilizer) without competition from other plants. A build-up of nitrates in the aquarium, although less toxic to the fish than nitrites,

BRACKISH WATER PLANTS

Both Java moss (*Vesicularia dubyana*) and Java fern (*Microsorium pteropus*) are suitable for a brackish aquarium, as are swordplants (*Echinodorus* spp.), which can be used to form a centerpiece. Other possibilities include eel grass (*Vallisneria spiralis*), which can be grown around the sides of the aquarium, as well as hornwort (*Ceratophyllum*). It should therefore be possible to create a suitable planted environment without too much difficulty.

can therefore create difficulties, although certainly in the case of mollies the fish curb the growth of the algae by eating it.

As to tank companions, there are other groups of fish, such as the now increasingly popular rainbow fish (*Melanotaenia* spp.), that occur like livebearers in a range of water conditions from freshwater through brackish. Egg-laying members of the Cyprinodontidae family, such as the popular American flagfish (*Jordanella floridae*) and the gold-spotted killifish (*Floridichthys carpio*), can also be considered. Other fish found in estuarine waters, including the mono (*Monodactylus argenteus*) and scat (*Scatophagus argus*), are possibilities, and widely available.

❶ American flagfish (*Jordanella floridae*), a suitable companion species for livebearers requiring a brackish water setup.

OTHER SPECIAL HOUSING NEEDS

Not all livebearers will thrive if kept in an aquarium full of water. The highly distinctive four-eyes (*Anableps* spp.) have distinctive requirements, not just with regards the relative salinity of their environment. If you want to keep these particular fish, you need to choose a rectangular tank and, since they rank amongst the largest of all popular aquarium livebearers, provide them with adequate swimming space. Additionally, the tank should be only half full. This is because these fish leave the water on occasions, so you need to provide them with a suitable platform for this purpose, located just above the surface of the water. It can be created quite easily by building a terrace out of slate at one end of the aquarium. Equally, the tank must be fitted with a secure hood to ensure that the fish cannot jump out of their tank.

For some species, the temperature of the water within the tank may need to be adjusted through the year. Examples include members of the family Goodeidae and others occurring in more temperate parts of the world, where the climate and hence the environment changes with the seasons. Temperature can be a particularly significant spawning trigger in certain cases, but it may not be feasible to adjust it if you have other fish in the aquarium—in such cases you may have to be prepared to set up a species-only tank. Reduce and then subsequently increase the water temperature gradually, over the course of a couple of weeks, rather than adjusting it suddenly, as this will be less stressful for the fish.

CHAPTER 4

Feeding Habits and Food

It is easy to keep the majority of livebearers on the prepared foodstuffs that are widely available for tropical fish, although there are now specific diets available for them too. Flake food is to be recommended, as it appeals to the natural feeding instincts of this group of fish by floating at the surface.

MOUTHPARTS

Although it may not be especially apparent in many cases, livebearers do have teeth in their jaws that also extend to the roof of the mouth. Their upturned lower jaw is relatively flexible and is set against the straight upper jaw, so they can rasp algae off a rock without great difficulty. The mouth itself is quite small and restricts the size of their prey. The lips are often slightly swollen, particularly in the case of those species that graze regularly on algae, helping to cushion them as their jaws rub on the rockwork colonized by these plants.

However, exceptions to this basic arrangement do occur, noticeably in the case of the pike minnow (*Belonesox belizanus*) and members of the halfbeak family (Hemirhamphidae). Pike minnows are the most predatory of all livebearers, and as such are equipped with much longer, tooth-filled jaws that enable them to seize and swallow their prey effectively.

⊙ Sailfin molly (*Poecilia velifera*). A protruding lower jaw helps livebearers to feed on algae.

THE DIGESTIVE TRACT AND DIET

The actual digestive system of live-bearers is not significantly different from our own. Food passes through the mouth and into the stomach, before proceeding from here down the intestinal tract, where the nutrients are absorbed into the body. The relatively long structure of their digestive system is an indication that most livebearers are omnivores although vegetable matter features quite prominently in their diet.

While feeding livebearers is generally straightforward, thanks partly to the development of specially formulated products, it is also important for their diet to be supplemented with natural foods. This helps to compensate for what may otherwise be a diet containing an excessively high amount of protein. Too much protein will be not be used to create muscle but instead converted to fat in the body, causing the fish to lose condition, and this in turn may affect their breeding performance.

The upturned mouth of most livebearers also gives an important insight into their feeding behavior, revealing that they seek food in the upper reaches of the aquarium rather than hunting around the base for it. This means that flaked food is a particularly suitable feeding option for this group, since it floats readily on the water's surface. If you offer no more than a pinch or so at a time, the livebearers will eat it up before it can sink to the floor and consequently pollute the aquarium. Any uneaten food left at the bottom can easily accumulate around rockwork and other tank décor, where it may be hard to see. It can then easily cause a sudden and serious deterioration in water quality thanks to its effect on the filtration system.

Within an aquarium, surface currents from the filtration system may sweep the food away too quickly. In such cases it can be useful to have a feeding ring, which keeps the food in one place and allows the fish to find it easily. Always feed the livebearers cautiously at first, just offering them a small pinch of flaked food at a time. This is necessary partly because the filtration system in a newly established tank is not functioning at maximum efficiency, and so any food left over is a particular threat to the fishes' well-being. It also takes the fish a few days to settle into their new surroundings, especially after the stress of the journey home, and this can affect their appetites. Before long, you will know almost exactly how much food to offer them in order to ensure that they have enough to eat without any waste.

⬆ Manufactured fish foods come in various forms. Moving clockwise from top left, cubes of freeze-dried tubifex, flake, and pellets.

GREENSTUFF

Since it takes time for green algae to grow in the aquarium, it is important to supplement the diet of the tank occupants with other sources of plant food. This is required not just for the health of the fish, but also keeps them from nibbling the new plants in the aquarium and so allows them to become established. You may want to offer fresh greenstuff for this purpose, particularly if you grow vegetables such as spinach or lettuce in your garden and these are free from chemical sprays that could otherwise be seriously harmful to the fish. The livebearers are able to nibble pieces off these leaves, especially if they are supported in a plastic clamp attached within the aquarium. This also makes it easy to replenish the leaves as necessary, before they begin to rot away. Alternatively, however, you can dice the leaves into very small pieces and drop them into a feeding ring. The ring helps to prevent them from drifting off around the tank, although ultimately the pieces will sink if they are not eaten.

Another useful supplement to the diet of many livebearers is frozen peas, which should be thawed before being dropped into the aquarium. They must be used with particular care, however, to avoid any accumulation of uneaten peas, and it is also a good idea to remove the outer shell as this is indigestible. Fresh peas can be equally palatable, although they can be made more digestible if they are parboiled first and allowed to cool.

The prepared foods based on *Spirulina* algae that are now available are also popular with livebearers. Special algal wafers offer another means of supplementing the vegetable component of the diet, and are appreciated by mollies in particular. Some flaked foods contain a higher proportion of vegetable matter than others.

COLOR FOODS

The prominent reddish-orange coloration of livebearers such as swordtails and platies (*Xiphophorus* spp.), not to mention guppies (*Poecilia reticulata*), can be influenced by their diet, particularly by a chemical known as carotene. Breeders have traditionally used foods that are naturally rich in this coloring agent to supplement the diet of their fish, usually carrot. The carrot needs to be boiled in a small volume of water, left to

STORAGE CONCERNS

A small tub of flaked food lasts a surprisingly long time, so check the expiration date on the pack to ensure that you do not continue using it once it is past. If you do so, your livebearers may be at risk of suffering from vitamin deficiencies, especially of vitamin C, which oxidizes readily. It is also vital that the food is kept dry, otherwise it is likely to turn moldy and has to be discarded. Keep the pack closed and store it in a relatively cool place to prevent any premature deterioration of the contents.

cool, and then chopped into very small pieces for the fish. Only a small amount is required.

As an alternative, there are special color foods on the market suitable for such fish, in the form of flake. These include specific guppy diets. Another natural way to improve the reddish coloration of some livebearers is by offering them live foods, notably daphnia (see below).

⬆ Colored food can be beneficial for livebearers that are predominantly reddish-orange, as in the case of this pair of swordtails (*Xiphophorus helleri* var.)

LIVE FOODS

Daphnia

Although they are sometimes confusingly known as water fleas, daphnia are in fact crustaceans and not fleas at all. They feed on tiny microbes in the water, which are sources of carotene, and hence can supply color to a diet. Feeding live foods, especially those of aquatic origin, is not without its dangers, particularly if they are collected from the wild. In the case of daphnia, other aquatic organisms present in the water in which the crustaceans have been collected can be hazardous to livebearers, especially fry, even to the extent of preying on them. There is also a significant risk of introducing diseases to the aquarium through this water.

Fresh aquatic live foods need to be purchased frequently as storage can present problems, and so you must be close to an aquatic store in order to obtain regular supplies. Even so, they have a short shelf life. When buying daphnia, always check the bag to ensure that the majority is alive, swimming around rather than lying dead in the bottom.

A long-term solution to obtaining a constant, fresh supply of daphnia is to set up your own breeding colony outdoors in a spare tank. All you need to do is allow the tank to fill with rainwater, and then introduce the daphnia here. During the warmer months of the year they should breed readily without problems, and you can net them using a fine sieve, transferring them to the aquarium. Only transfer relatively small numbers, which the livebearers should eat readily; otherwise, the daphnia may start dying in the aquarium, thereby affecting the water quality.

❶ Daphnia seen under the microscope. These aquatic crustaceans can be cultured at home.

Worms

Although they are very popular with livebearers, tubifex worms are even more hazardous than daphnia because of their origins. They inhabit stretches of water where there is high organic contamination, such as in the vicinity of sewage outflows. Tubifex therefore need to be viewed with caution, although they can be cleaned over a period of time by being left in a jar or tray under a dripping faucet. These worms cling together in such surroundings, forming a mat, and if they are not kept in running water their tank must be refreshed at least two or even three times a day. It is also important to store them in a cool, shaded spot outdoors, as they will soon die if exposed to bright sun.

Small chunks of the worms can be offered to the livebearers via a special tubifex feeder. This needs to be fixed onto the side of the aquarium just below the water level, and is usually held in place here by a rubber sucker. The livebearers cluster around the feeder, taking the worms out of it. The feeder prevents the worms from invading the gravel, where they split up and so are less likely to be eaten by the fish.

Prepared live foods

Partly because of fears over the health problems that can arise through the use of tubifex and other live foods, and also because of difficulties in their supply, alternative sources of invertebrate foods have now been created for the fishkeeping market. These include frozen live foods, which are supplied in small sachets that need to be stored in a freezer and thawed prior to use. If you only have a single tank of livebearers, to save waste it is possible to cut slivers off a frozen block with a sharp knife rather than thawing the whole lot. Frozen foods are relatively expensive, but the fish usually eat them. Gamma irradiation, as used to sterilize hospital equipment, is applied to this type of fish food. This eliminates any harmful bacteria and other microbes, so making the food much safer than if it was fed in an unprocessed state.

Freeze-dried live foods offer another possibility. These are sold in tubs and have no special storage needs, other than that they must be kept dry. This process entails freezing the live food initially, and then removing all the water by drying rather than heating it. The resulting foods retain their smell and flavor, so their palatability is not significantly affected. A wide range of items is available in this form, including tubifex, but avoid those that are likely to be too large for livebearers, such as river shrimp.

The latest innovation in the field of prepared live foods comes in the form of individual sterilized sachets, which allow you to determine just how much food to give your fish. The sachets do not need to be refrigerated, and the jellylike consistency of such products contains additional vitamins and minerals. Daphnia and bloodworm are now being sold in this form.

> ### LIVE FOODS AROUND THE HOME
>
> **Even a garden pool or water-butt can be a source of valuable live foods for livebearers over the warmer months in temperate parts of the world. Various midges and gnats are attracted to such places and lay their eggs here. It is then possible to scoop out the gnat larvae, or indeed bloodworms (so called because of their red coloration), which are the free-swimming stage in the lifecycle of midges. Simply leaving an old bowl outdoors over a period of time can establish a useful reservoir of such foods, at least during the summer. Since these live foods do not originate from an environment where fish are present, the likelihood of transmitting diseases is correspondingly lessened.**

Brine shrimp

The size of live foods is a particular issue as far as the fry of livebearers is concerned. In order to meet theheir protein requirements and ensure healthy growth, the fry require a relatively higher proportion of live food in their diet. Small daphnia can be used for this purpose, but many breeders prefer to supplement the food intake of young livebearers with brine shrimp nauplii instead, as well as with prepared foods.

As their name suggests, brine shrimp (*Artemia salina*) often inhabit shallow saltwater lagoons, which are prone to drying out. They produce eggs, which are simply deposited in the substrate, from where they are harvested. They are then packed and sold in airtight containers to exclude moisture.

↑ The nauplii of the brine shrimp (*Artemia salina*) are a good live food for livebearers.

⬆ Live food: mosquito (*Culex* sp.) larvae and pupae hanging at the water surface. There are also some swimming larvae beneath the water lily flowers.

There are various ways in which the brine shrimp eggs can be hatched, and special kits are marketed for this purpose. Basically, all you need is a large bottle or similar container that can be kept aerated, and some marine salt to add to the water in which the larval brine shrimp, known as nauplii, will hatch. The water should be kept at a temperature of around 77°F (25°C); hatching takes place after about 24 hours. The nauplii can then be sieved out of the solution and transferred to the aquarium. Care needs to be taken to prevent the fry from eating the eggshells of the brine shrimps, because these can cause a fatal blockage in their intestines. It may be safer simply to obtain shell-less eggs for hatching purposes.

Terrestrial live foods

Other live foods can successfully be cultured in the home, and also represent no threat to the livebearer's health through introducing aquatic diseases or parasites to the aquarium. A variety of small worms can be obtained in the form of starter cultures. These include microworms (*Panagrellus silusiae*), as well as whiteworms (*Enchytraeus albidus*), and grindalworms (*E. buchholzi*). Although they are not all sold by stores, worms of this type are available from live food suppliers that advertise in the fish keeping magazines.

Divide the starter group into smaller colonies. Place these in a plastic container, such as a clean margarine tub, that has been filled with a peat-based substitute, taking care to ensure that this does not dry out. Place a little bread soaked in milk adjacent to each group to act as a food source. Keep the culture in a relatively warm environment, topping up the food supply as necessary. Within about a month, it should be possible to harvest worms from the colonies for the fish.

In areas where wingless fruit flies (*Drosophila*) can be bred, these too can make a valuable addition to the diet of livebearers. Commercial kits and feeding media are available for these invertebrates, but a clean jar covered with a muslin top held in place with a rubber band will suffice, along with banana skins as a food source. Once the young fruit flies have hatched and grown to a reasonable size (usually about two weeks from setting up the culture), they can simply be tipped in small numbers onto the surface of the water in the tank, where they will soon be gobbled up by the fish. Don't use all the fruit flies at once, as it is useful to have more than one culture available.

MEAT

A food that was commonly given to livebearers in the past, but is less widely used today, is ox heart. There are fears that the fat level of this food is too high, and so it is a good idea to use only pieces that are visibly free of fat. Ox heart can be particularly useful for the predatory pike minnows (*Belonesox belizanus*). Thin wafers can be grated off a frozen piece and dropped into the tank one at a time for these fish. Any leftover meat soon causes a deterioration in the water quality and is likely to make the aquarium smell unpleasant, so use an aquarium cleaner to lift out any remains without delay once it is clear that the fish have lost interest.

VARYING THE DIET

There are clearly a number of feeding options when it comes to catering for livebearers. While it may be tempting to rely on prepared foods because they contain all the necessary ingredients to ensure the fish should stay healthy, do try to supply the livebearers regularly with other items to supplement their basic diet.

In the wild, the fish are likely to have access to a range of different types of food, and this may vary through the year. Greenstuff adds to the level of fiber in a fish's diet and can help to prevent obesity, which means that not only is it likely to live longer but also have a higher chance of breeding successfully. Live food has proved to be a useful breeding trigger, especially for those species that tend not to spawn so frequently in aquarium surroundings. It can also have beneficial effects on the coloration of the fish and their growth.

⊙ A magnified view of whiteworm (*Enchytraeus albidus*) in a culture. These small worms make a valuable addition to the diet of livebearers.

CHAPTER 5

Reproduction

The reproductive habits of livebearers have helped to ensure their popularity. The fact that females of many species in the group give birth to live young in the aquarium makes them easier to breed than egg-laying fish. In addition, the so-called "fancy" strains have a particular appeal to exhibitors, and can create a stunning impression in the home, as a group will look particularly striking when kept in the same aquarium.

BREEDING SUCCESS

All reproductive strategies have one aim in common: the continued survival of the species. Aside from the obvious differences in their breeding habits, the major feature that sets livebearers apart from egg-laying fish is that they produce far fewer offspring. However, their fry are obviously born in a much more advanced state of development, and thus avoid the perils faced by eggs, whose numbers are greatly reduced before they even hatch.

The first critical stage in the production of live offspring is the ability of the adult fish to mate successfully. This has been achieved in the case of livebearers by the modification of the anal fin into a gonopodium, which enables milt containing the male's sperm to be

🔻 Top-quality show guppies are highly-valued as brood stock, enabling breeders to develop their own strains of such fish. This strain has earned the informal name "super guppy".

introduced directly into the female's body.

The sperm is funneled into the female's body in the form of tiny microscopic packets, described as spermozeugmata, and up to as many as 3,000 are transferred as the result of a single mating. In the case of goodeids, the sperm are arranged with their heads attached to the mucus core of the spermozeugmata and their tails floating freely, although this arrangement is reversed in other species such as guppies (*Poecilia reticulata*).

An even more remarkable phenomenon is the way in which females are subsequently able to retain active sperm from the male fish in their bodies, so that they can give birth to a number of broods in succession, without having to mate again. The guppy has been known to produce as many as eight broods in this way, and may only need to mate once to remain fertile throughout its life. In order to be certain of the parentage of any offspring, it is therefore vital to start out with virgin livebearers.

> ### OCCASIONAL LIVEBIRTH
>
> **Internal fertilization is not confined exclusively to livebearers. Poeciliid *Tomeurus gracilis* females normally lay eggs, but on rare occasions they may retain some eggs within their bodies, where they subsequently develop so that the fry are born alive. The fact that this does not happen consistently is why it is described as facultative viviparity.**

REPRODUCTIVE HABITS

Livebearers themselves can broadly be split into two groups, based on their reproductive habits. The majority of poeciliids are described as being ovoviviparous. In such cases, the eggs are fertilized internally and then simply retained in the relative safety of the female's body until the young are ready to emerge from their eggs. There is no direct contact with the female through this period, and the young fish derive their nutriment direct from the yolk sac within the egg, just as occurs with egg-laying fish.

In the case of viviparous livebearers, including goodeids and certain poeciliids such as mosquito fish (*Heterandria* spp.), there is a much closer link between the female fish and her offspring. There is a direct physical connection between the two, the female nourishes the young while they are inside her body, rather like the situation for most mammals. This means that as the fry grow larger, so the female viviparous livebearer must find increasing amounts of food in order to meet the requirements of her developing brood.

The development process does vary, however—the eggs of four-eyes (*Anableps* spp.), for example, are fertilized while they are still in the ovary. Here they remain to undergo what is described as follicular gestation, whereby the yolk sac acts rather like a mammalian placenta, connecting the developing fry with their mother and allowing nutrients to be taken directly into their bodies. This method of absorption is particularly efficient in the case of *Anableps* compared with other viviparous livebearers, as reflected in the growth rate of the offspring. Studies have revealed that the weight increase through to birth in the case of members of this genus can average 298,000 percent, whereas the equivalent figure for mosquito fish (*Heterandria formosa*) is just 3,900 percent. To facilitate the process, the developing *Anableps* have specialized cells on their belly sac, described as vascular bulbs, which are in close contact with the maternal epithelium.

The way in which the fry of other viviparous species develop is significantly different. Both *Jenynsia* and goodeids display what is known as ovarian gestation, whereby their embryos migrate from the follicle to enter a cavity within the ovary. The young goodeids then grow so-called trophotaeniae from their anus. These long, thin cords, whose name literally translates as "feeding worms," are responsible for nourishing the young until they are born. They connect with the ovarian wall for this purpose and are usually clearly apparent for a short time after birth in goodeids. The situation is reversed in the case of *Jenynsia*, however, because the connection stems from the female. Outgrowths known as trophonemata extend from the wall of her ovary into the gills and mouth of the young, allowing the transfer of nutrients and gaseous exchange to take place.

SIZE AND SURVIVAL

Although giving birth to live young obviously precludes the production of potentially large numbers of offspring in a single brood, some livebearers have adapted to this challenge by breeding almost continuously. This is aided by the fact that females of all species,

◉ Livebearing provides relative safety and security for the offspring, but the size of the female places constraints on their number. Some livebearers exhibit superfetation, with ova that have been fertilized at different times developing in the uterus simultaneously. This green swordtail (*Xiphophorus helleri*) shows staggered development of viviparous embryos.

with the notable exception of goodeids, can store sperm.

Mosquito fish (*Heterandria* spp.) display a phenomenon known as superfetation to help compensate for their diminutive size (they rank among the smallest of all vertebrates). Instead of producing their young in a single batch, female mosquito fish give birth to just several fry every few days. This is possible because the young are at different stages of development within the female's reproductive system. As a consequence, mosquito fish fry are proportionately large at birth, being about a third of the size of their mother. This is particularly important because the size of the fry at birth is likely to have a direct impact on their chances of survival through the critical early days of life.

In other cases, eggs may start their development but not be fertilized until after the previous brood has been born. This is why female guppies have broods on a regular basis. Even so, their reproductive cycle is not fixed, as individuals have sometimes been recorded as breeding in the same way as *Heterandria*.

HYBRIDIZATION

The way in which livebearers interbreed with one another is regulated to some extent by the structure of the male's gonopodium, as described earlier (*see* page 62). Even so, it is not uncommon for related species to breed together successfully, particularly in aquarium surroundings. Intergeneric crosses have also been recorded, between *Poecilia* and *Limia*, for example, although the offspring of such pairings are often infertile.

As far as maintaining aquarium strains is concerned, particularly in the case of the rarer livebearers, it is important to ensure that the fish are housed in such a way that hybridization is not possible. It has been exploited commercially, however, to create a number of the most highly colored and widely kept livebearers, including many forms of swordtail (*Xiphophorus* spp.). Mollies, too, are well known for their ability to hybridize, as reflected by the case of the black molly (*Poecilia sphenops* var.), which is an entirely domestic creation.

In the wild, mating can have unexpected results, as emerged from a study of the Amazon molly (*Poecilia formosa*). The natural range of this species extends from southwestern parts of Texas southwards to northeastern Mexico, and it is always found in the company of related species, typically *P. latipinna* in the U.S., and both *P. mexicana* and *P. sphenops* in Mexico. However, close studies of the Amazon molly reveal that its population throughout its range was comprised almost entirely of female fish only. Yet these individuals were observed mating regularly with males of the other species living alongside them. This suggested that their offspring were hybrids, but on closer study a remarkable finding emerged, confirming that these mollies were the first ever unisexual vertebrates known to science.

The sperm from the other *Poecilia* mollies did not actually fertilize the eggs of the Amazon mollies: their eggs are highly unusual. Instead of containing the normal single set of genetic material on a chromosome, which then combines with that of the male, the eggs of Amazon mollies contain paired chromosomes, both of which derive from the female. Their offspring are therefore in effect clones.

It has subsequently emerged that the act of mating is still physiologically important for these fish, as it is necessary to trigger the development of the eggs themselves, even though it does not contribute genetically. As to how this remarkable reproductive arrangement developed is still unclear, but it appears that Amazon mollies first evolved about 100,000 years ago. It has been suggested that they themselves were originally the result of hybridization, between the sailfin molly (*P. latipinna*) and the Atlantic molly (*P. mexicana*). Certainly, crosses between these other species in aquarium surroundings have resulted in the breeding of mollies not dissimilar in appearance to *P. formosa*.

There is also the question of how the female Amazon mollies lure the males of other species to mate with them. Close studies of the mating behavior of the Amazon molly have shed light on this phenomenon. In the first place, they are more aggressive, seeking to interfere with normal conspecific matings (between members of the same species). It is also likely that an element of conditioning is involved as well, especially since Amazon mollies will school with

⬇ Liberty molly (*Poecilia sphenops*), one of the species that plays a vital part in ensuring the survival of the Amazon molly (*P. formosa*).

MYSTERIES OF THE MALE AMAZON MOLLY

In the wild, it has been estimated that the incidence of male Amazon mollies is typically about one in 10,000, which confirms that the species does actually still possess genes determining male gender and associated characteristics, although these are generally suppressed. By treating pregnant females with hormones, it is possible to induce male characteristics in their offspring. When apparently male fish are produced as a result of matings, they possess an extra chromosome as part of their genetic makeup. The fact that they have three rather than two chromosomes leads them to being described as triploids. However, the underlying process here is not fully understood, because all such "feminized" males bred in aquariums have proved to be infertile, yet studies involving wild triploid individuals have revealed that these fish are fertile. The wild triploids are able to produce offspring with an identical genetic makeup to their own, allowing the triploid characteristic to be retained within the population. It may be that by this means the male chromosome is effectively preserved within the population, so the potential remains for it to be reactivated in the future.

these other species. This makes it more likely that mating will occur, because the males choose receptive females in the school whatever their species, and do not apparently distinguish between them.

The effects of this relationship do not only impact the Amazon molly, but also affect the behavior of the sailfins toward one another. While female sailfin mollies instinctively prefer larger males, the act of a smaller male consorting with a female Amazon molly will in turn attract the female sailfin to that particular male. The consequences of associating with female Amazon mollies influences the behavior of male sailfins as well, because although they may prefer females of their own species, they will start pursuing a female Amazon molly more vigorously if another male has been observed with her.

Thus competition appears to encourage not only hybrid matings, but also matings of the species itself. Nor is copying of the mating preferences of other fish unique to these mollies, as it has been observed in guppies too.

Conditioning is clearly significant. When Amazon mollies were reared in association with sailfins, they subsequently displayed a preference for mating with this species, even if they could have chosen Atlantic mollies (*P. mexicana*) instead. This preference for the familiar was confirmed when the Atlantic mollies grew up with Amazon mollies, suggesting that early experiences are involved in determining mate preferences in members of this genus.

MATE CHOICE

The process by which female guppies choose their mates has been the subject of intense investigation. Mating in poeciliids is thought to be triggered by the release of estrogen, which acts as a pheromone (chemical message) to attract males to a receptive female. It is thought that the estrogen is detected by the sense of taste, which helps to explain why males often resort to nipping at the vent region of a receptive female prior to mating.

The mating ritual itself differs noticeably between different genera, serving to reflect characteristic differences in the structure of the male's gonopodium. Those with a long copulatory organ, including mosquito fish (*Heterandria* spp.), can insert this visually, and so there is little precursory courtship. In contrast, mating in livebearers that have short gonopodiums is a much more complex procedure, as their organ cannot be inserted visually. They do possess a well-developed gonopodial hood, however, which aids the positioning of the gonopodium for mating purposes. Livebearers with longer gonopodiums generally lack or have a much reduced hood, relying instead on sensory spines located on the underside of the third ray of the fin to help them make adequate contact with the female. In cases where mating is brief, the sperm packets are not usually passed into the female's body, but instead are deposited at her genital opening.

At the other extreme, contact is much more obvious in swordtails (*Xiphophorus helleri*), when the male actually clasps his mate directly with hooks present on his gonopodium. If one of these hooks is missing, then mating is less likely to occur, and the absence of both precludes a successful union. The way in which the pair subsequently parts after copulating is traumatic, with the male almost tearing himself free from his partner. This can cause injury and even blood loss in some cases. It has been suggested that the resulting trauma may make the female less likely to mate again until the inflammation has subsided, thereby increasing the likelihood that the male's sperm fertilizes the majority of her eggs. However, if two males mate almost simultaneously with a female, the likelihood is that the offspring will be of mixed parentage.

Once inside the female's body, the gelatinous sperm packages effectively dissolve within about 15

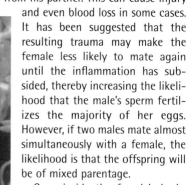

🔾 A male mosquito fish (*Heterandria* spp.) displaying its gonopodium to a female.

minutes, freeing the sperm. They normally effect fertilization over the course of five days. Those sperm that do not make contact with an egg will be stored within folds in the ovary and in the gonoduct. It is unclear how they manage to survive here for as long as two years, although they may be nourished by the outflow from sugars produced by the ovary. The presence of female hormones may also prevent the sperm from being destroyed by her immune system over this period.

It takes somewhere between 20 and 30 days on average following fertilization before the young are born, although this depends both on the species as well as the temperature of the water. In the case of female guppies, the gestation period lasts approximately 28 days at a water temperature of 77°F (25°C), but falls to just 19 days when the temperature is increased to 92°F (32°C). At the other extreme, breeding ceases once the water temperature falls to about 59°F (15°C).

The fry themselves are fully formed early on during this period. In the case of platies, the development process takes just five days; the remainder of the gestation period is given over to their growth. The presence of the so-called gravid spot, a bulge on female poeciliids, formed by part of the peritoneum (the lining of the abdominal cavity), is taken as a sign by breeders to indicate that they are carrying young. The spot becomes more apparent as the time for birth approaches and subsequently fades in prominence after the event.

GENDER DETERMINATION

Although young poeciliids are born in equal ratio of males to females, studies of adult populations in a number of localities, and involving various species ranging from platies (*Xiphophorus helleri*) to pike livebearers (*Belonesox belizanus*), have revealed that by the age of maturity there are typically more females than males in the

◐ A pair of courting guppies (*Poecilia reticulata*), with the smaller, more colorful male in the foreground.

⬆ A gravid
female black platy
(*Xiphophorus
helleri*), with a
characteristically
swollen body.

population. This can be explained not only on the basis that males are more colorful and therefore more conspicuous to predators—especially piscivorous fish—but that they are also more vulnerable to stress. This can apply in aquarium surroundings, too, just as in the wild where environmental conditions are less favorable. The fact that females take longer to mature than males also suggests that they have a longer lifespan.

This relative shortage of males is not a general problem with regards to the survival of these fish in any event, primarily because a single male can mate with a large number of females over a period. In addition, even if all the males were removed from the population, female poeciliids that had mated previously would still be able to continue producing offspring, thanks to their ability to store sperm. Ironically perhaps, it is the remarkable Amazon molly (*Poecilia formosa*) that is most likely to suffer from the absence of males. This is because these particular livebearers, comprising an almost entirely female population, must mate in order for their eggs to start developing (*see* pages 95–7).

The numbers of males produced in broods may also sometimes be affected by water temperature. According to research carried out with *Poeciliopsis lucida*, the percentage of male offspring increases significantly as the water temperature rises.

This may reflect seasonal changes that occur in the wild and affect the breeding patterns of livebearers in both temperate and subtropical areas. Food is likely to be more abundant and numerous during warmer months, and so the production of a greater number of males at this time possibly provides the opportunity for the population to grow more rapidly, especially as females take longer to mature.

OTHER REPRODUCTIVE TRIGGERS

Water temperature alone does not appear to be the sole trigger influencing reproductive activity, certainly in the case of the mosquito fish (*Heterandria formosa*). A falloff in daylight in southern Florida curbs the breeding behavior of this species here in the fall, and the combination of both increasing light exposure and temperature then serves to trigger breeding again in the spring.

Poeciliids occurring in tropical regions can show a response to changes in photoperiod, but other factors such as rainfall and the availability of aquatic live foods are also likely to be significant conditioning factors. Certainly, as far as the aquarium is concerned, increasing the quantity of live food in the diet often proves to be a successful breeding trigger with many species.

Females cease to have broods toward the end of their lives. They develop a rather emaciated appearance, which could potentially be confused with the signs of piscine tuberculosis, although the weight loss is not just apparent on the underbelly but also around the dorsal fin on top of the body. They can even undergo an apparent switch in gender at this stage as well, as the result of hormonal changes in their bodies following declining ovarian function. This phenomenon is most common in swordtails (*Xiphophorus helleri*), but has been recorded in other common livebearers as well.

BROOD SIZE

A number of factors influence brood size. It is certainly a good idea to allow females to remain in the company of males, simply because if they do not mate the number of young they produce declines over a period of time. This suggests that there is a falloff in the numbers of sperm carried within the body. In any event, the young born will owe their parentage to the male that mated most recently with the female.

Another factor affecting brood size is the size of the female: on average, larger females produce correspondingly more offspring. In the case of guppies (*Poecilia reticulata*), this finding has even been correlated using a fairly complex mathematical formula by Dr. Affleck, who devised a special breeding trap to prevent any of the young fry in his study falling victim to cannibalism as this would have seriously compromised the results. According to his research, it is possible to calculate the likely number of guppies (N) produced in a brood simply by ascertaining the length of the female's body, which is designated by the letter L in Affleck's equation:

$$N = 5.2L - 15.5 - (0.7L - 14)$$

THE BREEDING ENVIRONMENT

It is quite possible to leave the newborn livebearers in their aquarium, but within these surroundings many of the young fry are simply gobbled up by the other occupants, including their mother, which does not distinguish her young after having given birth to them. Those that do survive, however, won't be harassed once they are large enough to avoid being swallowed. Nevertheless, the number of young able to survive within the confines of the aquarium is almost certain to be much lower than in the wild, partly because there is far less space for them to hide from predators. In their natural environment young livebearers often move into the shallows, where they are largely out of reach of bigger fish. There is frequently plenty of cover available here as well, including leaf litter, other debris, and aquatic vegetation.

All that can be done to safeguard young livebearers in a community aquarium is to ensure that it is well planted, especially with densely growing plants such as Java moss (*Vesicularia dubyana*) so that the fry have some hope of remaining out of reach of the older fish. Regular feeding is also important, so that the adult fish are not forced to look for additional items to supplement their diet.

TRANSFER TO THE SPAWNING BOX

Restricting the movements of the female to a spawning box can be stressful for her. The stage at which she is caught and transferred is therefore critical—if she is moved too late, it is likely that she will abort her brood prematurely and they will then be unlikely to survive as a result. Once a female has produced young, it ought to be possible to estimate when another brood is due. Adult female swordtails (*Xiphophorus helleri*), for example, produce young every four to six weeks. Another guide that can be used is the appearance of the black gravid spot on the female's flanks, which is a clear sign that her young will be produced very soon.

Spawning boxes

Rather than leaving the young to fend for themselves, you may prefer to use a spawning box, a form of breeding trap in which they are kept in relative safety in the main aquarium. There are various designs available, but it is important to choose the largest model that fits your aquarium, especially if you need to accommodate bigger livebearers such as swordtails (*Xiphophorus helleri*). The boxes can be hooked over the side of the aquarium, so that they are kept in place and do not drift off.

Ideally, the female is transferred to the trap about a week prior to giving birth, and is usually confined to the top part of the unit, which has a false base. The fry can then escape out of her reach into the lower chamber, slipping through the grill. Once the female has produced her young, she can then be released back into the main tank so that the fry are left in the trap on their own.

There are a number of drawbacks to this setup, especially with relatively large broods. Feeding the young livebearers in a breeding trap can be very tricky, as you need to match their growing appetites adequately to the amount of food provided.

This is especially significant with no filtration system within the unit itself. Although time-consuming, regular (daily) water changes are likely to be essential as any deterioration in water quality could easily wipe out the brood.

⬆ A floating breeding trap in use. Breeding traps allow young livebearers to escape from their mother by dropping into the box body below.

Breeding tanks

In practical terms, there is actually little advantage in using a spawning box unless the main aquarium has a low stocking density. This is because it's not feasible to release the young into the tank itself once they have grown without overcrowding it. However, by establishing a breeding tank you can be sure that the young livebearers not only have the greatest likelihood of surviving safely, but also have adequate space to grow on.

A setup of this type does not have to be elaborate, and the tank itself is usually smaller than the main aquarium. It needs to incorporate a breeding trap, where the female can be confined until she gives birth. The young will then be able to slip out of the trap and away from her reach.

Once this has happened, the female can be returned to the main tank, and the trap can then be removed and the offspring left to be reared on their own. It is essential that the filtration system within the breeding tank is gentle in order to prevent the young being sucked up—as would happen with a power filter. A sponge filter is ideal in these surroundings, along with an undergravel filter if the tank itself does not have a bare base.

Alternative breeding setups

Other means of providing a safe refuge for newborn livebearers within a communal aquarium lie in creating a more natural environment, where the female can be restrained and the fry can escape from her quite easily. This can take the form of a larger breeding trap, which may simply be in the form of fine nylon mesh draped into the water of the aquarium. The young will then be able to slip out through the small holes in the mesh into the lower reaches of the tank. This provides a way of protecting the fry at first, after which the adult female and the barrier should be removed from the aquarium so that the young fish are left on their own. A setup of this type can also be particularly beneficial where the female livebearer does not produce her brood all at once, but has small numbers of offspring over a period of time, as it gives her more space than the amount provided by a commercial spawning box.

If you are breeding livebearers regularly, a permanently modified aquarium can be arranged quite easily for the purpose. The idea is to partition the tank using two sheets of glass, held in place with silicone sealant and angled in a slight V-shape so that there is a small gap between them of approximately ⅛in (3mm). This will be large enough to allow the young fry to slip through the barrier, but also serves to retain the adult fish on the other side of this divide. The rearing area should cover about a third of the volume of the tank. The remainder of the aquarium can be decorated normally, but the position of the foam filter is very important as the current in the water should be gentle, yet sufficient enough to steer the young fry through the gap in the glass and thus to safety. As a further precaution to safeguard the fry, the area housing the adult fish should be well planted to afford the young cover as they are driven by the current toward the other side of the partition.

⬇ A swordtail (*Xiphophorus helleri*) female from southern Mexico, with newborn young ejected among waterweeds.

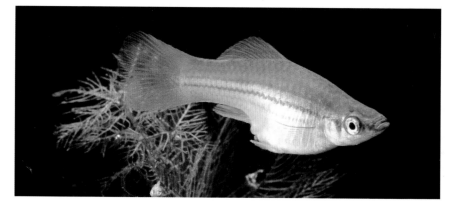

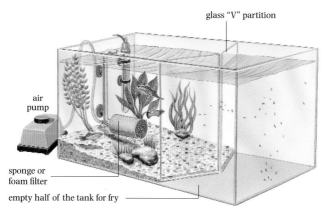

glass "V" partition

air pump

sponge or foam filter

empty half of the tank for fry

● Tank setup for livebearers with a "V"-shaped insert that has a gap to let the fry swim through. You can also split the tank with a wide mesh or perforated divider.

Once they are in the rearing chamber, the young livebearers are unlikely to swim back through the gap thanks to the power of the current. By the time they become stronger swimmers, they will have grown too large to slip back through the opening. By keeping this area of the tank free from any décor, you can ensure that the water will not become polluted by uneaten food. Any debris remaining here can easily be removed by careful use of an aquarium vacuum cleaner, although you need to take care not to suck up any fry.

Another possibility is to incorporate a perforated plastic sheet as a partition in a tank setup of this type. The holes should be of adequate size just to allow the fry through into the other part of the aquarium. However, this method often proves to be less effective than that using angled sheets separated by a gap.

REARING THE YOUNG

Special diets are available for newborn livebearers, although it is quite possible to rear them on flaked food—simply powder it through your fingers to create tiny particles. Many breeders also use live foods (especially small daphnia) for rearing purposes, but there is a risk of introducing other, more predatory, creatures such as hydra via this means, which may then attack the fry.

The young livebearers normally grow quite fast, especially if they are fed on a regular basis through the day. Larger foods can then be introduced to their diet, such as microworms. Some breeders recommend hardboiled egg yolk (reduce it to suitably fine particles by forcing it through muslin cloth), although it must only be offered in tiny quantities as any left uneaten will pollute the water very quickly. It therefore helps to feed the fry as frequently as possible. If you are at home through the day, offer smaller amounts every two hours or so.

The advantage of using aquatic live foods is that there can be a longer interval between feeds as these tiny creatures will hopefully live in the water without polluting it, unlike other foods, which soon start to decay. Brine shrimp nauplii (*see* pages 89–90) are especially useful because they survive well in brackish water. Although protein is the most important food group for young livebearers, it also helps to have some algae in the tank to supplement their diet.

GROWTH RATES

Within a group of fry, some may seek to monopolize the food supply and therefore start to grow at a faster rate. In such cases, a marked discrepancy in size will become apparent before long. This is often an indication that the group of young fish as a whole is not receiving adequate food. Within the group, however, there may also be some that are clearly handicapped, and these should be painlessly destroyed. A number of such deformed offspring is especially likely in the case of livebearers breeding for the first time, but if the problem persists in some lines it is a likely indication that the parental stock is too closely interbred. Abnormally curved spines are relatively common, as are twisted bodies.

The growth rate of young livebearers is fast, typically averaging about 0.007–0.01in (0.2–0.3 mm) per day, and is approximately the same whether they are living in the wild or are reared in aquarium surroundings. Up until the onset of sexual maturity, both sexes also have a similar rate of growth, although subsequently a marked divergence occurs. The females may then grow up to twice as fast as males.

Interestingly, it is not the presence of females that affects the growth rate of males, but rather the presence of other males. Where two males from the same brood are housed together, it has been shown that one grows faster and matures earlier than its companion. Nevertheless, the smaller individual continues to grow, and once it

● Black molly
(*Poecilia sphenops* var.)
female with its young
swimming over a
waterlily leaf.

reaches the size of its companion it then matures and keeps on growing, ultimately attaining a larger size than its companion. Such individuals have been termed "leap fish" by scientists, who have found that the phenomenon is common in platies (*Xiphophorus maculatus* and *X. variatus*). Further studies have shown that it is the result of the more aggressive nature of the males that mature earlier, probably reflecting their hormonal output. It does not occur in species where there are usually no signs of aggression between individuals, such as sailfin mollies (*Poecilia latipinna*).

The environment also exerts an influence on growth. In the case of the sailfin and other related species inhabiting brackish or saltwater environments, their rate of growth is typically slowed if they are kept in freshwater. Water temperature also plays its part, by increasing the fish's metabolic rate and encouraging its appetite.

The situation is not entirely straightforward, however, because there are also underlying genetic influences at work that have an impact on the size of the fish. Sexing young livebearers at an early age is therefore important in order to prevent unplanned matings. This is especially significant with platies, which are sexually precocious and may mate when they are 10 days old. It is unlikely that platy females will actually produce fry until they are about three months of age. The stage at which it is possible to sex livebearers varies, but for guppies it is typically about three weeks after birth.

⊙ Characteristics such as the enlarged dorsal fin seen in this variegated platy (*Xiphophorus variatus*) are the result of genetic mutations, which are then developed by means of a breeding program. This particular feature is not uncommon in various livebearers, often being described as the "hi-fin" form.

GENETICS

The way in which particular characteristics are passed from one generation to the next is controlled by the genes, which are present on paired structures called chromosomes, found in the nucleus of every living cell in the body. Under normal circumstances during

As far as livebearers are concerned, ornamental varieties have been created through selective breeding in four groups: guppies, mollies, swordtails, and platies. The changes in their appearance may be superficial, as in the case of variances in fin type, or it may be more profound. The coral platy (a form of *Xiphophorus maculatus*), for example, has a deep red body coloration, plus a deep-bodied appearance that results from an absence of vertebrae in its spine.

mating, genetic material from the female and the male (present in the egg and sperm) combines to form a new set of chromosomes. These have a direct influence on the offspring's appearance—for example, with regard to its coloration or fin type.

Such genetic changes can be preserved by careful breeding programs once the nature of the mutation responsible for the change has been identified. Mutations can be either recessive or dominant in their mode of inheritance, and this has a marked impact on the way in which the numbers of such fish can be increased by selective breeding. In the case of a dominant characteristic, simply pairing a livebearer displaying a characteristic of this type to another, irrespective of its genetic makeup, should result in a percentage of their offspring also displaying the dominant feature.

With a recessive trait, the situation is more complicated. In this case, offspring displaying the characteristic signs of the mutation are only likely to result if the partner chosen to breed with the parent exhibiting the characteristic also contains the relevant gene in its makeup, although this isn't physically apparent. This is a reflection of the ways in which chromosomes combine. The recessive gene is effectively hidden by its dominant compatriot on the other chromosome, unless two recessive genes come together in an individual. This then causes the particular recessive characteristic to be evident in that individual's appearance, or phenotype, rather than being masked by the corresponding dominant gene in the its genetic makeup, or genotype.

Selective characteristics

Although the appearance of male guppies (*Poecilia reticulata*) varies significantly thanks to marked differences in their fins, these changes are essentially not apparent in females. For best results, it is therefore important to obtain females of a known strain if you are interested in breeding particular types of guppies.

The buildup of colors can stem from several basic changes to the natural green-based coloration. So-called blond guppies have noticeably paler bodies as they lack the normal degree of melanism, or black pigmentation. Their eyes are still dark, however, in contrast to so-called albinos, which have pink eyes. There are also blue guppies, which lack shades of yellow and red in their makeup, and red ones.

Markings are a particular feature that has been developed in the case of platies (*Poecilia variatus*), and typically involve the caudal fin. There are one- and two-spot variants, where these particular markings are small, while others have markings may take the form of a crescent, or have a large rounded shape extending right down the caudal peduncle, described as moon-shaped. The crescent marking can also be combined with the moon, creating a patterning known as a complete moon. Platies with dark edges along the upper and lower edges of their caudal fins are called comets.

GERMAN SWORDTAILS

It has become something of a tradition with color varieties of livebearers to name them after the city in which the mutation in question was first developed. This began during the early years of the 20th century with swordtails (*Xiphophorus* spp.), and is reflected in the names of such strains of guppies as the Moscow blue and Vienna emerald. A number of the swordtail varieties that are now widely kept originated in Germany in the early 20th century, as commemorated by their names. The Frankfurt is one of the most common forms today, and is instantly identifiable by the contrast between the red front part of its body and the strongly demarcated black rear portion.

Berlin was the original home of another red swordtail, which is distinguishable in this case by its black spots. These fish must not be paired together because of the risk that their offspring will develop malignant melanomas, and so they are therefore bred with red individuals.

The Wiesbaden swordtail (*below*) has significantly more black on its body than the Frankfurt and Berlin varieties, and this extends right along its flanks, with the top and base of the body either red or green in color. Black pigmentation is even more pronounced in the Hamburg variety, where the entire body is black, offset with reflective scales, although the fins in this case are yellowish.

CHAPTER 6

Lifespan and Diseases

The downside of the fact that livebearers are generally prolific when breeding is that their lifespans are relatively short too. Most survive for just two or three years. However, aquarium fish almost certainly have a longer life expectancy than their free-living relatives, as they face fewer dangers. Indeed, provided that their environmental needs are adequately met, you should have few worries about their health.

LIFESPAN AND TEMPERATURE

In the case of some livebearers such as guppies (*Poecilia reticulata*), their surroundings do exert a direct influence on their lifespan. Studies have shown that guppies kept at relatively high temperatures close to 86°F (30°C) grow faster as youngsters but overall their lifespans are shorter, thanks to the increase in their body's metabolic rate. This is why breeders often keep young fish in slightly warmer water than adults, to encourage their growth, subsequently reducing the temperature in the tank once the fish are over three months old.

SIGNS OF AGING

⊕ If they are housed in community aquariums, mollies, such as this lyretail (*Poecilia latippina*), are particularly susceptible to fungal infections.

In their natural environment livebearers are likely to fall prey to a host of predators before they reach old age, but in aquarium surroundings old fish approaching the end of their lives may display signs of senility. This is often reflected by a loss of ability to swim effectively, and in the way in which such fish rest, often either right at the surface of the tank or lying on the substrate at the bottom. In such cases, however, their appetites are unlikely to be affected, although they may struggle to reach food as their swimming abilities become impaired. Disease will ultimately play its part in their demise, as weakened fish are vulnerable to fungal infection.

The microbes responsible for infections of this type are likely to be present within the aquarium water, but they rarely cause disease in healthy fish and only attack those that are weakened or injured. Such fish are more likely to succumb if they are kept in suboptimal water conditions, as this

places greater stress on their immune system. This is why mollies housed in community aquariums are especially vulnerable to fungus—in the wild they are found in brackish water, which appears to afford them some protection against infections of this type.

TREATMENT TANKS

It is always worthwhile having a small spare tank that can either be set up to quarantine new purchases, or converted to a hospital tank in order to treat a sick individual. Even if such treatment ultimately proves to be unsuccessful, removing an ill fish from the established

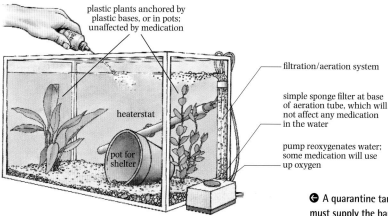

plastic plants anchored by plastic bases, or in pots; unaffected by medication

heaterstat

pot for shelter

filtration/aeration system

simple sponge filter at base of aeration tube, which will not affect any medication in the water

pump reoxygenates water; some medication will use up oxygen

➌ A quarantine tank must supply the bare necessities. While it is difficult to prove that adding plastic plants helps the healing process it seems logical that it might benefit a stressed or injured fish. Many livebearers, from swordtails to mosquito fish are used to sheltering in dense vegetation.

aquarium should help to lessen the risk that others will succumb to the disease. A hospital tank will also increase the likelihood of the sick livebearer's recovery, as the fish can be kept warmer and given appropriate treatment without being harassed in any way.

A setup of this type should be quite bare, with no substrate, although a retreat consisting of a flowerpot and plastic plant should be incorporated. This gives the fish somewhere to hide, so that it doesn't become stressed by being left exposed in the open.

A heater is needed, and it can be helpful to increase the water temperature slightly in this tank compared with that in the main aquarium itself. This is because the fish's immune system functions more effectively at a higher temperature, thus aiding its recovery. Filtration should take the form of a simple sponge filter. No activated carbon can be used in a filter in a tank where the fish are being medicated, simply because this chemical neutralizes the medicine. Nor is any lighting required, as this too could affect the fish's treatment and hamper its recovery.

SIGNS OF ILLNESS

Always take time to look at the fish in the aquarium every day when you feed them. You will then come to realize almost instinctively when one is off-color, simply by the change in its habits. You may find that the affected individual is not keen to eat, while the other tank occupants dart up to take their food without hesitation. An affected fish may also be less active than normal, hanging in the water or tending to hide away for longer than normal. The fish's color may alter, so that it appears to be either paler than usual or, sometimes, darker. Behavioral changes may also be apparent, in the way that the fish swims, perhaps brushing repeatedly against rockwork (suggestive of a skin irritation) or apparently swimming on the spot (a phenomenon described as shimmying).

When it comes to seeking help if your fish are ill, a knowledgeable fish store can prove very valuable, and should be able to offer both advice and a range of proprietary treatments. Alternatively, there may be a veterinarian in your area who is experienced in fish diseases and who can assist you accordingly.

FUNGAL DISEASES

There are many different fungi that can affect fish, although the type known as *Saprolegnia* is most commonly encountered in the case of livebearers. A fungal infection is especially likely to strike after an injury that has resulted in the loss of scales, possibly after a fight or through careless handling, as it can then gain relatively easy access to the fish's body. The early sign of this illness is likely to be a growth of what looks like cottonwool over the damaged tissue.

The immune system of most healthy fish is able to resist fungal infection, since they are constantly exposed to these organisms in the water, but any underlying illness is likely to leave them vulnerable. Early treatment can often prevent the fungal infection from being fatal, but it is equally important to try to identify the underlying cause of the problem. Commercially formulated fish foods now contain vitamin C to assist fish in resisting opportunistic infections of this type, by boosting their immune system.

Most fungal treatments have to be added to the water in the hospital tank, at the appropriate dilution, or the fish may need to be transferred from here to a separate container for treatment. Be sure to dilute the medication correctly, in accordance with the stated instructions, and do not leave the fish immersed in a treatment bath for longer than necessary. Such remedies can otherwise be harmful, particularly when a fish is already seriously weakened (this also applies in the case of other treatments). Do not forget to dip the net in a suitable solution of aquarium disinfectant after you have caught the sick fish in it, because it is likely to be contaminated by the fungus.

Fungus may not just strike on the body, and those livebearers with elaborate fins, such as delta-tail guppies, are especially at risk. A localized bacterial infection, causing fraying of the fins, can lead to a subsequent fungal infection here; the initial trigger in such cases is often poor water quality. Alternatively, the affected fins may have been nipped and damaged by other tank occupants. This is especially likely in a community aquarium housing a number of different species, and it may not always be easy to spot the offending fish, particularly if the attacks take place after dark. Damage to the fins is especially likely if the tank water is too cool, so it may also be helpful to increase the temperature slightly should a number of individuals be affected.

BACTERIAL DISEASES

Many infections are linked, in the sense that what may begin as a bacterial disease can lead on to a fungal illness if left untreated. Any reddening of a wound can be a potential indicator of septicemia (also known as blood poisoning), thanks to the way in which bacteria move through the body from the initial source of the infection. This is really serious, as vital organs may consequently suffer irreparable damage.

MOUTH FUNGUS

Rather confusingly, the condition often described as mouth fungus (to which guppies and black mollies are particularly susceptible) is not actually the result of a fungal infection. Instead, it is caused by a bacterium called *Flexibacter columnaris*. This ailment affects the mouth, causing a cottonlike growth that resembles fungus in appearance. Mouth fungus should always be suspected when a livebearer starts to hang near the water's surface, as the resulting obstruction interferes with the flow of water through its mouth and out across its gills, making it hard for the fish to obtain sufficient oxygen from the water.

Not all bacterial infections in fish are acute, however. Always watch for less obvious signs of bacterial illness, notably weight loss, which can be indicative of piscine tuberculosis. Some livebearers such as the porthole molly, *Poecilia (Mollienesia) latipunctata*, have a reputation for being especially susceptible to this infection, which can spread largely undetected in an aquarium when in its early stages. As guppies may be carriers of this disease, it is therefore inadvisable to mix them with porthole mollies.

A so-called "tucked-up" appearance, whereby the chest area takes on a concave appearance as the internal organs waste away, is a sign often associated with piscine tuberculosis, although the fish's appetite remains unaffected. Actual diagnosis of the illness is not necessarily straightforward, however, partly because of the range of possible symptoms. In some cases, an affected individual may have bulging eyes—a sign described as pop-eye, or exophthalmia. Nodules may also be evident under the skin. In such cases, affected fish should be euthanazed by a vet to prevent them from suffering further.

The mycobacteria responsible for piscine tuberculosis are passed out in the infected fish's droppings, and so can spread easily to the other occupants of the aquarium. Unfortunately, there is no treatment for this illness, so removing any suspected cases from the aquarium without delay will most effectively safeguard the health of other fish in the tank.

Regular water changes are important in helping to guard against general bacterial illnesses, notably minor infections of the fins. These are often described as fin rot and cause the fins to take on a ragged appearance. Provided that the water conditions are improved, this alone may be sufficient to ensure that the fins regrow without problems in due course. However, medication may also be advisable to prevent any risk of the infection spreading or of contamination by fungi.

● Sailfin molly (*Poecilia velifera*) with exophthalmia (pop-eye) as well as a fungal infection on a bruised lower lip.

PARASITES

There are many different types of parasite affecting fish, but the one thing they all have in common is that they have a detrimental effect on fish health and can even prove fatal in some cases. Piscine parasites can be subdivided into two categories, depending on whether they live inside or

outside the fish's body. The latter group, described as ectoparasites, is the most significant as far as livebearers are concerned.

Ich, or white spot

There are several types of microscopic protozoan ectoparasite that can cause serious illness and that are likely to spread very rapidly within the confines of the aquarium. They often result in intense irritation, so much so that the fish tries to overcome its discomfort by rubbing its body repeatedly against the rockwork and other décor in the tank. The most common of these parasites is *Ichthyophthirius multifiliis*, which causes the illness often simply known as "ich," or alternatively as white spot because of the appearance of the infection. It is especially prevalent in black mollies, but is also often encountered in guppies.

Ich can easily be recognized by the presence of white spots on the fish's body. These cysts soon rupture, each releasing many hundreds of tomites. These are the free-living form in the parasite's

↑ Orange-tailed goodeid (*Xenotoca eiseni*) with white spot. This weakens fish, leaving them more vulnerable to other infections as well.

⚠ PISCINE TUBERCULOSIS AND HUMAN HEALTH

If you have any cuts on your hands, there is a possibility that the mycobacteria responsible for piscine tuberculosis could invade your body, typically causing an unpleasant swelling at the entry site, although the effects might possibly be more serious if you have a depressed immune system. You can easily eliminate any risk of acquiring this infection by wearing a pair of rubber gloves whenever dipping your hand into the aquarium, which is a sensible precaution in any event. This not only protects you but also protects the fish in case you have any chemical residue on your hands that could do them harm. Even nicotine from tobacco can be potentially dangerous under these circumstances.

lifecycle, which then progress to attack other fish. The damage to the fish's skin leads to secondary infections caused by bacteria and fungi. White spot can infect livebearers in an aquarium repeatedly, which will soon result in their demise unless they are treated.

The best thing to do may be to remove all the fish to a separate treatment tank, and then raise the water temperature in the established aquarium slightly (bearing in mind the requirements of any plants growing here). This has the effect of speeding up the parasite's lifecycle, and means that if the free-swimming tomites do not find a host within a day or two they will die, and so the source of the infection is eliminated. In the meantime, the fish themselves can be treated. By removing them from the main tank, you can be certain that the concentration of tomites in their new surroundings will be significantly reduced at first, giving them a window for recovery while they are treated. Furthermore, there is no risk that a dye-based treatment, such as methylene blue, will permanently stain or discolor the silicone sealant in the main tank, as may otherwise occur. Bear in mind though that these parasites can easily be spread via water droplets on catching nets, and so to avoid cross-infection it is therefore a sensible precaution to have a separate net for each aquarium.

Velvet disease

Another parasite that is similar to white spot is velvet disease. Again, the organism responsible—*Oodinium* in this case—spreads through the water, multiplying rapidly and weakening the fish. This time though, the skin of affected livebearers assumes a velvetlike texture, sometimes with tiny gold-dust speckling. Similar treatments to those recommended for white spot should be adequate in this case, but mortality can be high, especially if young fry are infected. The parasites grow significantly once they have attached to the fish's body, anchoring themselves in place here by a rootlike structure. *Oodinium* often strikes the gills as well, causing the fish to have serious breathing difficulties.

Gill flukes

Another more localized parasitic problem that can affect the gills is gill flukes (*Dactylogyrus*). They anchor themselves in place by tiny hooks, which damage the delicate structure of the gills and can cause severe inflammation. Although barely visible to the naked eye, these parasites can easily be spotted with the aid of a hand lens.

The traditional treatment of gill flukes is immersing affected individuals in baths of dechlorinated water and formalin, but more recently the drug praziquantel has been proven to give good results

in place of formalin. Neither method is guaranteed to eliminate gill flukes in the short term, however, because their eggs may be dispersed within the aquarium, subsequently hatching and reinfecting the fish. This can obviously be a source of worry, and emphasizes the need to quarantine livebearers for two weeks or so to ensure they are healthy, before reintroducing them to the aquarium.

Skin flukes

Gyrodactylus, or skin flukes, are also found in livebearers and are often the cause behind the shimmying behavior seen in guppies in particular. Hooklike appendages anchoring them to the fish are again the reason for the irritation they cause. Unfortunately, although they may be more conspicuous than gill flukes, their reproductive rate is phenomenal. This is because young flukes are actually sexually mature at birth, and there may be up to three subsequent generations contained within a single infected fish. A combination of a proprietary aquarium treatment plus baths for affected individuals should soon serve to eliminate these parasites. Praziquantel appears to be equally as effective in killing skin flukes as gill flukes.

Intestinal worms

Livebearers are also vulnerable to infection by the intestinal worm *Camallanus*. Poor growth in the case of young fish is one of the most typical signs, thanks to the way in which these parasites gnaw at the lining of the intestinal tract with their strong jaws, resulting in hemorrhaging and anemia, which can lead to death. Their presence may be confirmed by the appearance of one of these worms (which measure about 0.4in, or 1cm in length) trailing out of the

◑ An anchor worm (*Lernaea* sp.) attached to a guppy (*Poecilia reticulata*). These parasites resemble threads of cotton hanging off the side of the fish. They are not commonly encountered in livebearers. There are proprietary treatments to dislodge anchor worms.

vent, resembling a piece of red cord. This should not be confused with constipation, where darker droppings may hang out of the vent in a similar fashion but subsequently break down easily.

Veterinary advice should be sought regarding treatment for *Camallanus* infestation, and medicated food is often required to treat these parasites. While it is possible for livebearers to acquire the infection by cannibalism, the more common route is often through contaminated live foods. *Camallanus* itself produces larval offspring, which are consumed by crustaceans such as *Cyclops*. Once the livebearers feed on infected live foods, so the larvae can complete their development, maturing into adult worms in the gut.

NON-INFECTIOUS ILLNESS

⊕ Any abnormal swelling of the body, often raising the scales close to the underparts, is described as dropsy. However, this is a symptom associated with various health problems, rather than being an illness itself. There can be a number of causes, but treatment is often problematic.

There are several unrelated conditions livebearers may occasionally suffer from, the cause of which may not always be obvious. An example of such a condition is bloat, or dropsy, although in this case its appearance is very distinctive: the scales become raised away from the body, creating what is sometimes described as a pinecone effect. Bloat may be the result of an intestinal disorder, but there is little that can be done as far as treatment goes.

Swim bladder disorders are most often seen in corpulent livebearers such as balloon mollies, and are apparent when the individual encounters great difficulty in regulating its buoyancy effectively. The exertions of the fish weaken it, and so transferring it to a small tank where the water is relatively shallow should bring some relief. A sudden fall in the water temperature can sometimes result in swim bladder disorders, as may pressure caused by an inflammation of neighboring internal organs. It may be possible to

overcome the most extreme effects of this problem, but the long-term outlook for affected livebearers is poor.

One of the worst things that can happen in fishkeeping is to discover that a number of the aquarium occupants have died suddenly, and that the surviving fish here are also showing signs of serious ill-health. Such an event is almost certainly likely to be related to a change in their environment. This could occur if you simply forget to use a dechlorinator when carrying out a partial water change, or it may result from the presence of other chemicals in the water. Copper from new waterpipes has been implicated in some cases of this type.

It is always important to check the water conditions carefully, although bear in mind that something as simple as overfeeding the fish for a period of time can have serious consequences. A surge in ammonia or nitrite can prove fatal, and will require a rapid, extensive water change without delay in the hope of saving the surviving fish. This may not be sufficient to save all of them, especially if they have already been severely weakened.

A surprising number of products in use in the home can be deadly to livebearers. Among the most dangerous are flea sprays for dogs and cats, as well as bug killers of any type. The fact that the spray is used in another room will not necessarily prevent a toxic concentration from accumulating in the water, as the particles can be drawn in through the tank's air pump. If this occurs you must remove the surviving fish to another tank Diluting the existing water in the tank will not guarantee the survival of the remaining fish, as only a tiny trace of poison of this type can be lethal to them. Keep buckets and other equipment used for cleaning and filling the aquarium exclusively for this purpose, to avoid introducing deposits of potentially deadly household chemicals.

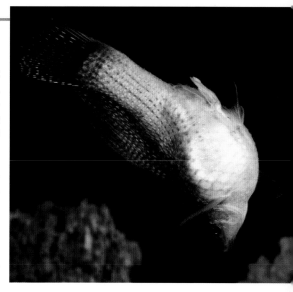

● Swim bladder disorders have various causes, but in all cases, an affected fish will have difficulty in maintaining its position in the water, with its organ of buoyancy affected.

MELANOMA TUMORS

Although not of great significance to fish keepers, some species—and *Xiphophorus* livebearers in particular—display differences in their genetic susceptibility to cancer, and as a result have been used in laboratory investigations into this ailment. Ordinary swordtails (*X. helleri*) and platies (*X. maculatus*) are normally very resistant to developing tumors, but when these two species are hybridized the resulting offspring are much more likely to develop skin tumors known as melanomas. The reasons for this are linked to an increase in the quantity of black pigment on their bodies. There is no treatment in such cases, and while some of the *Xiphophorus* offspring die before maturity, others will survive long enough to breed. A similar condition has been reported in the Cuban limia (*Limia vittata*), where yellow pigment is more intense than normal. This condition can be linked with a type of tumor known as a xanthoma, which (as with melanomas) is not transmissible to other fish in the aquarium.

CHAPTER 7

Popular Livebearers

FAMILY GOODEIDAE

★ BUTTERFLY GOODEID

Ameca splendens

Distribution: Mainly at the source of the Río Teuchitlán, and also in the Río Ameca in Jalisco, Mexico.

Size: Males grow to 2.3–3.2in (6–8cm), while females average 2.8–5.5in (7–12cm).

Form: Stocky body, with a dorsal fin that is located quite far back. This fin is especially prominent in males, and has been likened to the wing of a butterfly. These goodeids are silvery-white overall, suffused with shades of blue, green, and yellow depending on the light, and have a black band running down the body. There is a black subterminal band and yellow edging to the caudal fin. Females lack the iridescent colors of males and the solid bands, instead displaying stripes on the bodies.

Diet: Omnivorous but must be given adequate greenstuff alongside prepared foods.

Natural habitat and behavior: The river sections where these goodeids are found in the wild are only 5ft (1.5m) in depth and 20ft (6m) in diameter. Dense plant growth is present in some areas, and the water temperature is typically around 81–90°F (27–32°C).

Aquarium conditions: Good lighting is important to encourage plant growth, including algae. The water must be quite soft and well filtered, with a neutral pH. Butterfly goodeids are not aggressive toward other fish, including members of their family, but males often have brief disagreements among themselves. Pregnancy is prolonged at lower temperatures, lasting over eight weeks under such conditions. It takes approximately six months for sexual maturity to be reached. Young females have small broods, comprising as few as five individuals, and often their offspring may be slightly misshapen and may also vary quite noticeably in size. Subsequently, once they are older, female butterfly goodeids may produce 30–40 normal fry at a time. The young fish will have the visible remains of their umbilical cords attached to them for the first 36 hours of life.

⭐ RAINBOW GOODEID

Characodon lateralis

Distribution: Upper Río Mezquital in Durango, Mexico.

Size: Males attain a body length of 1.1–1.6in (3–4cm), while females average 1.3–2.2in (3.5–5.5cm).

Form: As its name suggests, this is one of the most colorfur species in the family. It has yellow underparts, with the remainder of the body having an olive-green background color. There is a pale bluish suffusion enhanced by reflective scales on the flanks of males, which are more colorful overall than females—reds and yellows are apparent on the males' bodies, hence the common name of rainbow goodeid. The dorsal fin is located just in front of the caudal fin. Both these fins and the anal fin are reddish-brown nearest to the body, with an outer ring of yellow and a terminal black band. Females are relatively dull in appearance, with more obvious black blotching on the sides of their bodies, and smaller, duller abdominal fins.

Diet: Eats a varied diet, in which vegetable matter, including green algae, should be prominent.

Natural habitat and behavior: Occurs in clearwater springs where there is some vegetative

cover. Water temperatures here vary widely, although typically are 64–81°F (18–27°C), and the rapid flow means there is little opportunity for nitrate levels to rise in these surroundings.

Aquarium conditions: The tank setup should have a dark substrate and incorporate a range of both rooted and floating plants. There should be good illumination to encourage algal growth, and efficient filtration to maintain water quality, coupled with frequent partial water changes. Rainbow goodeids, which are generally retiring fish, are not the easiest livebearers to maintain successfully and are best kept as a trio of one male and two females. They have also gained a reputation for being susceptible to piscine tuberculosis. The water in their tank needs to be moderately hard with a mildly alkaline pH close to neutral. Females give birth to broods of anywhere between five and 20 offspring, which are born after a gestation period lasting 55 days. In many broods, males outnumber females by five to one, which may be linked somehow to their environmental conditions. Mature females reproduce at eight-week intervals.

Goodea atripinnis

Distribution: Mexico, with the large nominate race being found in León, Alberca in Guanajuato's Valle de Santiago, and Río Ameca, Jalisco.

Size: Males can be as large as 4.7in (12cm), while females of the nominate race measure nearly 8in (20cm). In other races, such as *G. a. gracilis*, they may only grow to barely half this size.

Form: Up to five subspecies have been identified, separated both on the basis of their size and differences in coloration. Males have orange-brown underparts, although this is more yellowish in the dominant males. There is bluish suffusion on the flanks, while the remainder of the body is brownish. Females tend to be of a more consistent yellowish color overall, although their fins assume a blackish hue when the fish are in good condition.

Diet: Omnivorous, eating both prepared foods and live foods, including small earthworms. A vegetable component to their diet is essential.

Natural habitat and behavior: These black-finned goodeas occur in highland areas, where the water temperature may be in the range of 59–75°F (15–24°C).

Aquarium conditions: Medium-hard, slightly alkaline water, with a temperature of 68–75°F (20–24°C) suits these fish well. There are no discernible differences in the requirements of the different subspecies. They need a large tank to take account of their size, and should not be mixed with smaller companions, or larger ones with elaborate fins, as they have a reputation for fin-nipping. Black-finned goodeas are thus more commonly housed in a species-only setup, certainly for breeding purposes. They need plenty of open space for swimming, plus a well planted section within the tank. The water needs to be well filtered, and partial changes of up to a third of the total volume every two weeks or so are recommended. Females give birth approximately 55 days after mating, producing 15–60 young measuring about 0.8in (2cm) in length. Young goodeas may themselves start breeding when they are four months old. Mature females can reproduce every six to eight weeks.

FAMILY ANABLEPIDAE

⭐ FOUR-EYED FISH

Anableps anableps

Distribution: Ranges widely from southern Mexico to northern parts of South America.

Size: Males typically average 6–7in (15–18cm), whereas females measure 9–12in (23–30cm).

Form: Highly distinctive, surface-dwelling fish with prominent eyes that are located on the top of the head. The pupil in each eye is divided in two, so as to permit vision both under and above water simultaneously. The body is grayish-brown with five dark horizontal stripes, which vary in clarity. Underparts are white. Dorsal fin is located far back, near the caudal fin.

Diet: Prefers floating live foods, but takes prepared foods from the surface as well.

Natural habitat and behavior: Lives in shallow water, even emerging occasionally onto surrounding wet ground to seek food. Often rests on top of sand banks and similar submerged items. Able to jump well to avoid danger, and frequently encountered in

brackish water. Usually found in areas with a muddy bottom, where there is plenty of waste matter and algal growth.

Aquarium conditions: Four-eyed fish should be housed in a covered aquarium, in brackish water that has a specific gravity reading in excess of 1.011. The water temperature should be relatively cool, at about 77°F (25°C), and the level in the tank must be relatively shallow—do not fill it to the top. The aquarium itself needs to be roomy, and must incorporate adequate swimming space for these large fish. Rest platforms should be created from well-supported rockwork to allow the fish to bask out of the water, as they do in the wild. Cleanliness is important for their well-being, to the extent that some breeders do not use any substrate but instead rely on a power filter to keep the tank clean, along with regular water changes. The gestation period lasts some 20 weeks. The resulting broods often comprise less than six large offspring, which will each be over 1in (2.5cm) long at birth.

FAMILY POECILIIDAE

⭐ GUPPY (MILLIONS FISH)

Poecilia reticulata

Distribution: Northern South America, in Guyana and Venezuela; also present on neighboring Caribbean islands, including Trinidad, the Netherlands Antilles, the Leeward Islands, the Windward Islands, St. Thomas, and Antigua. Occurs in adjacent parts of Central America, too, as far north as southern Mexico. Has now been introduced to various other localities around the world.

Size: Males grow to about 1.2in (3cm), whereas females can reach 2in (5cm).

Form: Pointed head and elongated body. Wild forms are far less colorful than their domesticated counterparts. Females are naturally shades of gray or brown, with grayish-white underparts, while males are brighter in appearance, displaying patches of yellow, red, blue, green, and black coloration, depending on the population. The most widespread natural patterning is the "peacock eye," usually present on the caudal peduncle and so called because of its similarity to the markings on the tail of a peacock, with a dark ring surrounded by another color. The fins of the wild guppy are also far less elaborate than those of today's domesticated forms, but they sometimes display hints of the features that have since been emphasized by selective breeding. These can include the presence of a slight extension or "sword" on the otherwise rounded caudal fin, as well as a slight pennant shape on the dorsal fin.

Diet: Omnivorous, and easy to cater for in aquarium surroundings, as they eat prepared foods

⬇ Triangletail 'nigrocaudatus' (*Poecilia reticulata* var.)

⬆ Snakeskin triangletail (*Poecilia reticulata* var.)

of all types readily, as well as small live food. Vegetable matter is important in the diet and can help to maintain their coloration.

Natural habitat and behavior: Occurs in a wide range of habitats, from shallow ditches and pools to streams, rivers, and lakes. The water temperature in these different localities can vary quite markedly as well, in the range of 68–82°F (20–28°C), and some populations have even been found in brackish water.

Aquarium conditions: Guppies are relatively undemanding aquarium occupants, which, together with their attractive coloration and social natures, helps to explain their tremendous popularity worldwide. There is also keen interest in exhibiting fancy examples of these fish. Although they are quite adaptable, guppies will thrive best at a water temperature of 70–77°F (21–25°C), with a pH on the alkaline side of neutral, up to 8.5. A slightly brackish environment may be recommended, especially for wild stock, as this is likely to prove less adaptable than domesticated strains of guppy.

Breeding is straightforward, with the female producing her offspring approximately 24 days after mating. A typical brood comprises between 10 and 40 fry on average, although nearly 200 have been recorded. After mating once, females can give birth to repeated broods, which may be produced every four to six weeks on average. The aquarium itself should be densely planted, otherwise fry born here are likely to be eaten before they can grow large enough to survive within the group.

The female displays no recognition toward her offspring after producing them, but by keeping all the guppies well fed you will help to ensure that the young have the greatest likelihood of survival. The other option is to transfer the female to a breeding trap in a separate tank, returning her to the main aquarium as soon as she has given birth. The young guppies are just 0.02in (6mm) at birth, but grow rapidly and will be able to breed by the age of three months. Males tend to mature slightly faster than females. A special fry food for livebearers can assist the rearing of young guppies at first, along with crumbled flaked foods and brine shrimp nauplii at a later stage.

Poecilia sphenops var.

Distribution: Does not occur in the wild.

Size: Males are typically around 2.4in (6cm) in length, and the larger females average about 3.2in (8cm).

Form: Distinctive matt black coloration over the whole body distinguishes these fish from other mollies.

Diet: Omnivorous, but vegetable matter should feature significantly in their diet. They eat flaked and other prepared foods.

Natural habitat and behavior: These fish were originally created as the result of a program carried out during the 1930s by a breeder in New Orleans called Crencenty. He selected predominantly melanistic (black) forms of the pointed-mouth molly, which ranges from Texas right down through Central America as far as Colombia in northern South America. Other crosses were subsequently made, improving the vigor of these mollies, using *P. petenensis* to create the black Yucatan strain. The

Atlantic molly (*P. mexicana*) may also have played a significant role, but DNA studies are now needed to unravel the precise ancestry of today's strains of black molly. The range of such fish now available, all distinguished by their characteristic coloration, extends to hi-fins (with an enlarged dorsal fin), lyretails, and even balloon mollies (with a swollen body).

Aquarium conditions: Black mollies should be kept in slightly brackish water that is also alkaline and medium-hard. A concentration equivalent to a maximum of 0.13oz salt per gallon (1g salt per liter) will be sufficient, and the water temperature should be maintained at 77–82°F (25–28°C). These fish are very susceptible to white spot (*see* pages 115–16), and as this can spread easily within the confines of an aquarium, look carefully at all the fish on offer prior to any purchase. Females may produce anywhere from 40 up to 300 offspring, but they should not be moved to a separate accommodation late during their gestation, as this is likely to result in the young being aborted.

★ SAILFIN MOLLY

Poecilia latipinna

Distribution: Southern South Carolina, south to the eastern coast of Mexico. Introduced to other localities worldwide, including Saudi Arabia.

Size: Males grow to approximately 3.1in (8cm), whereas females are slightly larger, averaging about 3.5in (9cm).

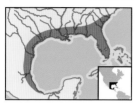

Form: The distinctive feature of these mollies is the large, tall, dorsal fin seen on the male. Their natural background color is olive-green, which is lighter on the underparts. There is reddish patterning running in rows down the sides of the body, extending to the fins. The more dominant, mature males display orange coloration on their chests. The dorsal fin is similarly colored, with blue and black spots, while the caudal fin is blue with red edging, although these fins are less brightly colored in females.

Diet: Omnivorous, and although it eats live foods readily it also feeds on algae. Interestingly, young fish fed predominantly on live food mature rapidly, but do not attain as large a size as those reared on a varied diet that includes more vegetable matter.

Natural habitat and behavior: The male sailfin molly uses its elaborate dorsal fin for display purposes. These fish occur in a range of waters from freshwater through to saltwater, while in various regions there has been natural hybridization with *P. mexicana*.

Aquarium conditions: Brackish water is usually recommended, and the temperature itself should be relatively high, in the range of 79–82°F (26–28°C). Algal growth should be encouraged, and there must be clear areas for swimming. The aquatic vegetation should be chosen to reflect the prevailing water conditions, and should also be strong enough to overcome being nibbled by the mollies. Good choices include Java fern (*Microsorum pteropus*), as well as *Vallisneria* spp. Floating plants with trailing roots are used as a refuge by young sailfin mollies, although a separate breeding tank is preferable. Females typically produce 10–60 offspring per brood.

Xiphophorus helleri

Distribution: Extensive range through Central America, from Río Nautla in Veracruz, Mexico, southward to Belize and Honduras.

Size: Variable, although males typically have a body size reaching 5.9in (14cm), with their so-called "sword" (a projection on the caudal fin) measuring an additional 1.6–3.1in (4–8cm), although these figures can vary significantly even within populations. Females (which do not display the sword) grow to 6.3in (16cm) overall.

Form: Narrow, streamlined appearance that is emphasized by the swordlike projection on the lower edge of the male's caudal fin. Females are typically slightly less colorful than males, with a rounded caudal fin. The natural coloration of these livebearers varies widely, depending on their locality. There are naturally occurring blue varieties, as well as green and red forms that are found together in Río Atoyac, and a speckled variety from Veracruz in Mexico. Speckled variants have also been documented from the Río Belize. The distinctive five-striped form, another Veracruz endemic, is restricted there to the Río Sontecomapan.

All the different variants tend to have limited distributions, so every effort should be made to keep pure strains of these wild forms. Selective breeding has also led to the development of various well-established commercial strains, including the red swordtail, which has striking orange-red coloration. Some, like the tuxedo form, display black markings, which in this case cover approximately two-thirds of each side of the body. Others have been created with modified fins, such as the lyretailed form. A number of these ornamental swordtails are not of pure descent, and are the result of hybridization with other related fish, such as the variable platy (*X. variatus*).

Diet: Omnivorous, consuming a wide range of foods including flaked and freeze-dried diets. Also eats thawed frozen foods.

Natural habitat and behavior: This species occurs in localities from highlands down to sea-level, usually inhabiting fast-flowing streams as well as rivers, often where there is established dense covering of vegetation. The water temperature is typically around 79°F (26°C).

⬇ Red tuxedo swordtail (*Xiphophorus helleri* var.)

⬆ Marigold needle swordtail (*Xiphophorus helleri* var.)

Aquarium conditions: Not difficult to maintain, but a relatively large, well-planted aquarium is important, featuring rockwork and other retreats. These will provide areas where male fish can hide without being challenged by the dominant male. Although ideally swordtails should be kept in groups comprising a single male with several females, be sure to have at least four males if you are housing several together. This will give them adequate opportunity to bicker collectively, rather than having a weaker swordtail bullied by a more dominant individual. As a result of their rather aggressive nature, these fish may unfortunately prove to be rather disruptive in a community aquarium.

Swordtails are athletic fish by nature and can jump well, so their aquarium must be well covered. Good aeration is also important, to mimic the effects of turbulence in their natural habitat, and partial water changes are required in order to keep the nitrite levels low. The water should be slightly alkaline and soft to medium-hard in terms of its chemical composition.

The swordtail's gestation period lasts around four weeks, and the number of young born is quite variable. It can be anywhere from just 20 up to 200, although as a guide, larger females have bigger broods. The young need to be removed from the main aquarium as soon as possible and reared on their own, although preferably the female should be transferred beforehand to a separate breeding tank to give birth. Her offspring are then free from persecution, especially by the male, which would otherwise be almost inevitable in the main aquarium. Small live foods are valued for rearing purposes. The young swordtails develop quite slowly, and even under optimal conditions they may not be sufficiently mature to breed until they are approaching a year old.

Xiphophorus maculatus

Distribution: Río San Juan, Veracruz, Mexico, south along the eastern side of Central America to Belize, Honduras, and Guatemala.

Size: Males grow to approximately 1.4in (3.5cm), whereas females can reach 2.4in (6cm).

Form: Quite stocky, with a high back. Platies display marked regional variation in coloration, with the males within a population invariably being more intensely colored than the females. There is often a blackish spot visible at the base of the caudal peduncle, and the belly is usually whitish. In the case of males occurring in the Río Papaloapan, Veracruz, the black coloration extends right down the sides of the body. By way of contrast, another population of these platies from the Río Coatzacoalcos is red, and so not surprisingly it has been possible to create a number of brightly colored varieties by selective breeding. Different localities in the same region may be home to what are clearly separate populations—for example, a grayish-brown variety is also present in the Río Coatzacoalcos.

Diet: Omnivorous, but flaked foods can be used as a staple diet. Do not forget to offer vegetable-based foods regularly. Platies also browse on algae.

Natural habitat and behavior: Occurs in relatively shallow, standing areas of water, including marshes, ponds, and pools, rather than in flowing water. Sometimes, the depth of water may be only 2in (5cm), barely covering the fish. As a result, these shallow bodies of water warm up quickly under the tropical sun, typically reaching temperatures in excess of 86°F (30°C).

Aquarium conditions: Platies are usually maintained at a relatively high temperature, about 77°F (25°C). They should be kept in waters that are relatively still and they do not need such frequent water changes as some livebearers. Females produce batches of 20–80 fry about four weeks after mating. The young are mature by the age of five months.

⭐ MOSQUITO FISH (DWARF LIVEBEARER; DWARF TOPMINNOW)

Heterandria formosa

Distribution: Eastern Seaboard, from southeastern parts of North Carolina via eastern and southern parts of Georgia to Florida. Extends along the Gulf Coast, to the vicinity of New Orleans, Louisiana.

Size: Males grow up to 0.8in (2cm), while females can reach 1.4in (3.5cm).

Form: These fish are the smallest livebearers, and also rank among the smallest of all vertebrates. Their most obvious feature is a dark brown line running down each side of the body, which is otherwise of an olive-gray shade. A dark spot is clearly visible on the dorsal fin, which is yellowish-red, as is the anal fin. The depth of yellow coloration on the fins varies, depending on the individual population.

Diet: In spite of their name, these fish require greenstuff in their diet as well as insect life of suitable size. They can be maintained on prepared foods so long as these are augmented with small live foods. Green algae growing in the tank provide a valuable additional food source.

Natural habitat and behavior: This species inhabits shallow areas of both fresh and brackish water, which are often choked with vegetation. The most striking biological characteristic of mosquito fish is that females give birth to small numbers of fry over a long period, rather than producing them in a single batch. This phenomenon is known as superfetation.

Aquarium conditions: A tank for these fish needs to be densely planted, partly to reflect their natural habitat and also to provide good cover for their young. Because of the way in which they produce their offspring almost constantly, there is no point in setting up separate breeding accommodations for females, but removing the fry to separate quarters for rearing can help to maximize their chances of survival. The optimum water temperature is 24–27°C (75–81°F), although they can live at temperatures as low as 61°F (16°C).

Gambusia holbrooki

Distribution: Found naturally on the Eastern Seaboard, from New Jersey south to Florida, and west to central Alabama.

Size: Males may grow up to 3.5cm (1.3in), while females measure 1.6–2.4in (4–6cm).

Form: Very similar to the closely related species known as *G. affinis*, of which it is sometimes considered to be a subspecies. Slightly smaller in size, grayish in color, often with a diamond-checkered outline across the body, and with lighter underparts. Dark markings are apparent on the dorsal and caudal fins of both sexes, while some male fish have significant areas of black on their bodies. This results in a mottled appearance, and they may even be completely black, a condition described as melanistic.

Diet: Should be offered a carnivorous diet as they feed mainly on live foods in the wild. Provide suitable live foods, such as gnat larvae, when available.

Natural habitat and behavior: Few fish are more adaptable than this species, as they can survive in water temperatures close to freezing right up to 86°F (30°C) or more. Populations of large mosquito fish have been introduced to many localities outside their natural range—including parts of Mexico, the Middle East, Africa, and Asia—as a means of controlling the aquatic stages in the breeding cycle of mosquitoes. They are also found through areas of southern Europe, from Portugal and Spain east to Hungary and the former Yugoslavia.

Aquarium conditions: Typical water temperatures should be in the range of 68–82°F (20–28°C), and there is no need to add salt. Even in temperate areas, it is possible to acclimatize these fish successfully to living outdoors in a pond over the summer at least, but great care must be taken to ensure that they cannot escape. Brood size can vary from 10 to nearly 80 fry, with mature females producing offspring every five to eight weeks on average.

⭐ HUMPBACKED LIMIA (BLACK-BARRED LIMIA)

Limia nigrofasciata

Distribution: The northern part of Lake Miragoane and the Étang Saumâtre pool in Haiti, on the Caribbean island of Hispaniola.

Size: Males can grow as large as 2.2in (5.5cm), while females typically measure 2–2.5in (4–6cm).

Form: Both sexes have between seven and 12 vertical black bars running down the sides of their bodies, sometimes also with intervening black markings between them. Depending on the light, there may be a turquoise sheen on the body, although the underlying ground color is an olive-yellow and the fins are yellowish. Males also have yellow underparts, whereas those of females are white. There is a distinctive difference in body shape between the sexes, with the characteristic hump of the male fish becoming increasingly prominent as they grow older. The sharp keel that extends from the anal and caudal fins in the males further emphasizes this difference in body shape. The black streaking on the dorsal fin of males also becomes denser with age, and in some cases is almost totally black.

Diet: Requires a diet based both on vegetable flaked food and small live foods as it is omnivorous by nature. A varied diet is important for breeding success.

Natural habitat and behavior: Occurs in both brackish conditions and freshwater, and is most common in relatively shallow areas where aquatic vegetation is abundant.

Aquarium conditions: Quite adaptable, and can be included in a community tank alongside non-aggressive companions. Humpbacked limias prefer relatively hard, neutral, or slightly alkaline water, heated to 75–82°F (24–28°C). The water temperature may be significant in influencing the gender of the fry, as more male fish tend to be produced in warmer conditions. A typical brood comprises between 10 and 60 fry, which will themselves be mature around four months of age. Adult fish tend not to cannibalize their offspring, although individuals do differ in this regard.

Limia melanogaster

Distribution: The Caribbean island of Jamaica.

Size: Males of this species may grow to 1.5in (4cm) or so, while the larger females can vary in the range of 2–2.5in (5.5–6.5cm).

Form: The body shape of these limias is quite slender, and the head is correspondingly small. Their underlying color is grayish-brown, but in adult fish (particularly males) there is a characteristic bluish suffusion that is most apparent in a well-lit aquarium. The black area evident on the belly of the female is distinctive, while males of this species have more intense yellow coloring at the base of the caudal fin. Both sexes display black banding on their flanks, extending from about midway down the body to the base of the tail. Dominant males can usually be identified by pronounced black coloration on their dorsal and caudal fins as well. As they have been kept and bred in aquariums for nearly a century, domestic strains of these limias now tend to be more colorful than their wild counterparts.

Diet: Omnivorous. Plant matter such as algae is important in their diet, and they also consume small live foods such as brine shrimp nauplii.

Natural habitat and behavior: Black-bellied limias are widely distributed across Jamaica, inhabiting shallow, fast-flowing streams that are largely free from vegetation. They may also be found in flooded marshy areas where the water can be very shallow, often just 4in (10cm) in depth, and consequently heats up rapidly during the daytime.

Aquarium conditions: Hard, alkaline water conditions are necessary. Water movement is also important in a tank housing these limias, as are areas of open space in which they can swim. Planted areas at the sides will provide cover for the young during the crucial early days of life, but adult fish are not highly predatory toward their fry, especially if they are well fed. Females are quite prolific and may produce broods of 20–60 offspring every month.

★ PIKE LIVEBEARER (PIKETOP MINNOW)

Belonesox belizanus

Distribution: Occurs naturally in eastern Central America, from Veracruz in southern Mexico down to Guatemala, Nicaragua, and Honduras. Also introduced to Florida.

Size: This is one of the larger livebearers, the males typically measuring up to 4.5in (12cm) long, while the females are much larger at as much as 8in (20cm) in length.

Form: Reminiscent of a pike (*Esox lucius*) in appearance, as befits the predatory lifestyle of these fish. Narrow body shape, with teeth in the powerful jaws. Relatively plain coloration, with a yellowish-brown body, paler underparts, and variable black speckling on the flanks. There is a larger black spot at the base of the caudal fin, and usually some black markings on the dorsal fin of male fish.

Diet: Carnivorous, preying not just on invertebrates but also on smaller fish. Can be persuaded to take both previously frozen and freeze-dried foods.

Natural habitat and behavior: Pike livebearers inhabit stretches of water where there is dense aquatic vegetation, lurking here with the aim of ambushing smaller fish. They are found mainly in coastal waters, but also farther up river systems where the flow of water is quite slow. The body coloration of these fish is influenced by mood—for example, they can turn completely black when they are excited.

Aquarium conditions: These fish must be housed in well-planted tanks that mirror their natural environment; in bare tanks, they prove very nervous by nature. Hard water conditions, alkaline pH, and a water temperature of 75–81°F (24–27°C) suits them well, along with the addition of some marine salt in order to create a slightly brackish environment. Breeding is straightforward, and between 40 and 100 fry are born, typically just 4½ weeks or so after mating. Small live foods such as daphnia may be provided as rearing foods for the young, and despite reports to the contrary, it is not unknown for females to prey on their own offspring.

Alfaro cultratus

Distribution: The eastern side of Central America, in Panama, Nicaragua, and Costa Rica.

Size: Males typically grow up to 2.4in (6cm), while females may reach 4in (10cm).

Form: This species has a slender body, while the two rows of scales that extend along the lower edge of the caudal peduncle are reminiscent of a knife in shape—hence its name. The basic ground color is olive-gray, with paler underparts, and there are green and bluish hues evident on the flanks. The fins are colorless, but watch for dark edging to the caudal fin, which develops in older individuals.

Diet: Small live foods such as daphnia are preferred, but they will also eat flaked foods.

Natural habitat and behavior: These livebearers inhabit fast-flowing streams and are correspondingly powerful swimmers.

Aquarium conditions: A water temperature of 75–82°F (24–28°C) is recommended, and the water should be soft with a pH around neutral. Although these fish are not usually encountered in brackish waters, beneficial results have been claimed for the addition of a little sea salt to the tank water. Clean water conditions are important for knife livebearers, reflecting the flowing water of their natural habitat. In suboptimal surroundings, these livebearers succumb readily to bacterial ailments. Regular water changes every two weeks are therefore recommended, with as much as a third of the volume of their aquarium being replaced at this stage.

Effective planting is also necessary, because knife livebearers can be nervous by nature. They can be mixed with nonaggressive fish that require similar water conditions, but are often kept in a single-species setup. The gestation period in the case of these livebearers is short, the females giving birth just over three weeks after mating. Brood sizes are quite small, numbering between 10 and 30 offspring, which can be reared on brine shrimp nauplii.

FAMILY HEMIRHAMPHIDAE

⭐ WRESTLING HALFBEAK

Dermogenys pusillus

Distribution: Southeast Asia, from Myanmar (Burma) and Thailand, south across the Malay Peninsula and to the Sunda Islands, Indonesia.

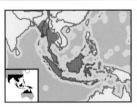

Size: Males grow to a length of 2.2in (5.5cm), while females are up to 1in (2.5cm) longer overall.

Form: Five different subspecies of this halfbeak have been described through its wide range. The body shape of these fish is long and narrow, but their most characteristic feature is their toothless lower jaw or "beak," which extends well beyond its upper counterpart. There are slight variations in color, reflecting regional differences: the nominate race is grayish-olive, with paler underparts. Mature males are mostly brightly colored, with a golden sheen on their bodies and a slight bluish tinge on their underparts. The anal and dorsal fins are red at their bases, becoming yellow toward the edges.

Diet: These fish are mainly carnivorous, preferring a diet of live foods—especially items such as wingless fruit flies, which they can eat at the water's surface. Try to encourage them to eat some prepared foods in order to supplement their vitamin intake and to prevent the incidence of stillbirths. They can usually be persuaded to eat some flaked food without difficulty.

Natural habitat and behavior: Halfbeaks live near the surface in a variety of different localities, ranging from flowing freshwater to brackish environments. As their name suggests, the males are territorial and battle each other fiercely.

Aquarium conditions: These halfbeaks are shy and often rather nervous, especially in unfamiliar surroundings, and so should be kept in a rectangular tank that offers plenty of space for swimming and is also well planted to provide cover. Floating plants are important to give these fish a sense of security, especially as they can easily injure their protruding lower jaws by swimming forcefully into the side of the tank. The water temperature should be 75–80°F (24–27°C), and the environment is usually slightly brackish. Males must be housed apart from one another to prevent fighting. Broods consist of 10–30 fry, which must be fed small live foods if their rearing is to be successful.

Further Reading

Alderton, David. *The International Encyclopedia of Tropical Freshwater Fish*. New York: Howell Book House, 1997.

Alderton, David. *The Complete Guide to Fish Care*. London: Mitchell Beazley, 1998.

Andrews, Chris. *A Fishkeeper's Guide to Fish Breeding*. London: Salamander Books, 1986.

Andrews, Chris, Excell, A., and Carrington, N. *The Manual of Fish Health*. London: Salamander Books, 1988.

Baensch, Hans A. and Riehl, Rudiger. *Aquarium Atlas* Vols 1–3. Melle: Baensch, 1987, 1993, 1996.

Banister, K. and Campbell, A. (eds). *The Encyclopedia of Aquatic Life*. New York: Facts on File Inc., 1995, 1998, 2004.

Dawes, John. *Livebearing Fishes: A Guide to Their Aquarium Care, Biology and Classification*. London: Blandford, 1991.

Dawes, John. *Complete Encyclopedia of the Freshwater Aquarium*. Ontario: Firefly, 2001.

Hieronimus, Harro. *Guppies, Mollies, Platys—A Complete Pet Owner's Manual*. New York: Barron's, 1993.

Hiscock, Peter. *Creating a Natural Aquarium*. Dorking: Interpet Publishing, 2000.

Houde, Anne E. *Sex, Color, and Mate Choice in Guppies*. Princeton: Princeton University Press, 1997.

Jepson, Lance. *A Practical Guide to Keeping Healthy Fish in a Stable Environment*. Dorking: Interpet, 2001.

Kempkes, Michael and Schafer, Frank. *Livebearers and Halfbeaks*. Morfelden-Walldorf: Verlag A.C.S. GmbH, 1998.

Lambert, Derek. *A Practical Guide to Breeding Your Freshwater Fish*. Dorking: Interpet Publishing, 2001.

Meffe, Gary K. and Snelson, Franklin F. (eds). *Ecology and Evolution of Livebearing Fishes (Poeciliidae)*. Englewood Cliffs: Prentice Hall, 1989.

Parenti, Lynne R. A Phylogenetic and Biogeographic Analysis of Cyprinodontiform Fishes (Teleostei, Atherinomorpha). *Bull. Amer. Mus. Natur. Histor.* **168**: 335–557, 1981.

Sandford, Gina. *The Questions and Answers Manual of the Tropical Freshwater Aquarium*. Oxford: Andromeda, 1998.

Scheurmann, Ines. *Aquarium Plants Manual*. New York: Barron's, 1993.

Scott, Peter W. *A Fishkeeper's Guide to Livebearing Fishes*. London: Salamander Books, 1987.

Wischnath, Lothar. *Atlas of Livebearers of the World*. Neptune: T.F.H. Publications, 1993.

Web Sites

http://www.livebearers.org/ This is the home page of the American Livebearer Association. Essential for photos and information about this group of fish, and contacting fellow enthusiasts, as well as how to join the ALA.

http://lists.aquaria.net/fish/livebearers/ A discussion forum about livebearers and their care.

http://www.guppyland.net/articles_livebearers.html A useful general site about guppies.

http://www.aquarium-dietzenbach.de A German site, with information in English too. General, but useful for photographs of new species and details about established ones too.

http://www.aqualink.com Certainly this currently represents one of the largest fish keeping Web sites. A useful starting point when seeking further information.

Glossary

Acidic A reading on the **pH** scale below 7.0.

Adsorb The way in which molecules passing through a filter may adhere to a porous surface such as carbon.

Algae Microscopic plants present in water, which can coat glass, rockwork, and other surfaces in the aquarium, especially under conditions of high light intensity.

Alkaline A reading on the **pH** scale measuring above 7.0.

Anal fin Unpaired fin in front of the vent.

Andropodium Term sometimes used to describe the **gonopodium** of halfbeaks (Hemirhamphidae).

Biotope The fish and its natural environment.

Blackwater extract Commercially available preparations that mimic the soft, acidic water conditions prevalent in the Amazonian region and elsewhere, also helps to stimulate breeding behavior.

Brackish Water conditions that are more saline than freshwater, but are not as salty as seawater itself. Typically encountered at the mouths of estuaries.

Brood The number of young produced by a female at one time.

Caudal fin The tail fin.

Chemical filtration Typically describes the use of activated carbon to remove harmful substances from solution.

Chromosomes The strands on which the genes are located in the nucleus of cells.

Crown The center of a plant, from where new growth occurs.

Dechlorinator A product which removes harmful chlorine from local water supplies, making it safe for the fish.

Dorsal fin The prominent fin which lies farthest forward on the upper area of the back.

Dropsy Abnormal swelling of the body, which may have infectious or non-infectious causes.

Family A taxonomic grouping of fish consisting of several different **genera**.

Fancy A strain of fish selectively bred for characteristic features, such as coloration or fin shape.

Filter bed The medium, such as gravel, through which water passes as part of the filtration process.

Fins Projections on a fish's body that it uses for locomotion and display, as well as mating in some cases.

Flake Very thin wafer-like manufactured food for fish that floats well on the water surface, being very thin.

Free-swimming The stage at which young fish start to swim around for the first time.

Fry Young fish.

Genus A related group consisting of one or more species.

GH Reflects the general or permanent hardness of a water sample. Unaffected by boiling the water.

Gills The major means by which fish are able to extract oxygen from the water. They are located just behind the eyes on each side of the head.

Gonopodium The modified anal fin associated with male livebearers, which is used for inseminating females.

Gravid The swollen appearance of female fish that reveals they are about produce young.

Hard water Water that contains a relatively high level of dissolved calcium or magnesium salts.

Heaterstat Combined heater and thermostat unit for aquarium use.

Hybridization The successful mating of two different species together, which results in so-called hybrid offspring.

Ichthyologists Those who study fish.

KH A measure of temporary hardness, resulting from bicarbonates or carbonates dissolved in the water, which can be reduced by boiling.

Lateral line A sensory system running down the sides of the fish's body, which allow it to sense vibrations in the water.

Length Measurement of a fish is usually carried out in a straight line from the snout to the base of the caudal fin, which is itself excluded from the figure.

Livebearers Fish that reproduce by means of internal fertilization, with females retaining their eggs in the body.

Mechanical filtration The direct removal of waste matter by filtration, which effectively sieves it out of the water.

Mouth–brooder A fish that retains its fertilized eggs in its mouth until they hatch, and may also allow its young back there for a period afterwards to escape danger.

Mulm The debris that can accumulate on the floor of the aquarium.

Nauplii The larval stage in the life-cycle of the brine shrimp *Artemia*, cultured as a rearing food for young fish.

New Tank Syndrome Describes the potential for sudden death of aquarium occupants resulting from a fatal build-up of ammonia and nitrite in a newly-established tank where the filtration system is not working effectively.

Nitrogen cycle The breakdown of toxic ammonia produced by the fish through nitrite and less toxic nitrate, which is used by plants for healthy growth.

Nocturnal Fish that are active after dark.

Omnivorous Eating both plant and animal matter.

Operculum The movable flap which covers the **gills**, and allows water to flow over them.

Ovoviviparity Livebearing reproductive strategy that consists of internal fertilization with most of the embryos' nourishment originating from the egg **yolk sac**.

Pectoral fins Those located on each side of the body behind the gills.

Pelvic fins The fins present in front of the **anal fin**.

pH The relative acidity or alkalinity of a solution, based on a logarithmic scale, so each unit change represents a tenfold alteration in concentration, with pH 7 being neutral. Low values reflect increasing acidity; higher figures indicate a progressively more alkaline solution.

Pharyngeal teeth Sharp projections used for rasping food, located in the pharyngeal region of some fish.

Photosensitive Affected by light.

Photosynthesis Process by which plants manufacture their nutritional requirements using light.

Plankton Microscopic plant and animal life in the water.

Power filter A filtration unit that incorporates its own pump to drive water through the unit.

Predation The killing and eating of live prey.

Quarantine The complete isolation of newly acquired fish for a period of time, to ensure they are healthy, before introducing them to other fish; or the isolation of a sick fish.

Rays Bony framework that provides structural support for the fins.

Scales Protective covering present over the bodies of most fish.

Soft water Water that is low in dissolved salts, as typified by rainwater.

Speciation The process and selective pressures that lead to the creation of a **species**.

Species A group of fish that closely resemble each other and can interbreed.

Spermatopodium Term sometimes used to refer to the **gonopodium** of males of the family Goodeidae.

Standards The specified criteria that are used by judges when assessing particular varieties of fish at shows.

Strain A line of fish specifically developed for particular characteristics such as color or fin shape; may be named after the breeder responsible for creating it.

Substrate The floor covering in the aquarium or the base of the fish's natural habitat

Superfetation The presence in the uterus of two or more fetuses developing from ova fertilized at different times; common in members of the *Poeciliopsis* genus, and other livebearer genera.

Swim bladder The fish's air-filled organ of buoyancy.

Taxonomy The science of identifying fish and unraveling their relationships.

Tomite The free-swimming, infective stage of the microscopic parasite that causes white spot.

Toothcarps Members of the order Cyprinodontiformes, comprised of both livebearers and their egg-laying relatives, often called killifish.

Trophotaeniae Outgrowths from the vent area of goodeid embryos (family Goodeidae) through which they obtain nourishment during their early development.

Undergravel filter A plate filter that fits right across the bottom of the aquarium.

Vent Ano-genital opening behind the anal fin.

Viviparous Giving birth to live offspring (noun: viviparity).

Yolk sac Source of nourishment for fry prior to and immediately after hatching.

Index

Page numbers in *italic* refer to illustrations.

African tiger lotus 76
aging 110–11
Alfaro 39–40, 70
  A. cultratus 39, 136, *136*
  A. huberi 40
alfaro's livebearer 39, 136, *136*
algal growth 82–3
Allodontichthys 29
  A. hubbsi 29
  A. polylepsis *29*
Alloophorus 29–30
  A. regalis 29
  A. robustus 29
Allotoca 31
  A. dugesii 30
  A. maculata 31
  A. regalis *30*
amarillo 33, *33*
Amazon molly 95, 96–7, 100
Amazon sword 74
Ameca 30–1
  A. splendens 30, *30*, 120, *120*
American flagfish 83, *83*
Amistad gambusia 19
Anablepidae family 9, 37–9, 61, 123
Anableps 37–8, 58–9, 83, 93–4, 123, *123*
  A. anableps 9, 38, 83
  A. dowi 26, 38, *38*,
  A. microlepis 9, 38
anchor worm 116–17
angelfish 58
aquariums:
  acrylic 65
  algae in 82–3

brackish water in 70
breeding in 102–5
filtration systems 68–70
glass 65–6
gravel 72–3
heating control and temperature 70–2, 83
history of 6–7
lighting 72
positioning 66–7
rocks in 77–8
sealants 65–6
size 67
special needs 83
stands 67
stocking density 68
woodwork 77–8
aquarium plants 74–9
  choosing 74–6
  brackish 82
  floating 77
  planting 75–6
  schemes 74
Ataeniobius 31
  A. toweri 31
Atlantic molly 96, 97

bacterial diseases 113–15
balloon molly *60*
Barbus tetrazona 58
barred topminnow 51–2, *51*
Beaufort's halfbeak *57*
Belonesox 40
  B. belizanus 40, *40*, 62, 74, 84, 91, 99, 135, *135*
Betta splendens 58
Big Bend gambusia 18–19, *18*
black molly 126, *126*
black-barred limia 133, *133*
black-barred livebearer 51–2, *51*

black-bellied limia 134, *134*
blackfin goodeid 28, *28*
black-finned goodea 122, *122*
black-seam mosquito fish 42, *42*
blond cobra guppy *49*
bloodworms 88, 89
blue-tailed goodeid 31
bogwood 78
Brachyrhaphis 41
  B. roseni 41, *41*
brackish water 70, 82
breeding 63, 92–109
breeding tanks 103–4
brine shrimp 89–90, 106
brood size 101
bulrushes 19
butterfly goodeid 30–1, *30*, 120, *120*

Camallanus 117–18
camouflage 16
Carlhubbsia 41
  C. kidderi 41
  C. stuarti 41
cartilaginous fish 8
Ceratophyllum 82
Chapalichthys 31–2
  C. pardalis 31
Characodon 32
  C. garmani 32
  C. lateralis 32, 121, *121*
chlorine 81
cichlids 14
Cnesterodon 42
coelacanth 8
color and marking 108–9
coral platy 108
Crenicichla alta 15, *16*
crescent goodeid *37*

daphnia 87–8, 89, 105
De Filippi 6
Dermogenys 55–6
  D. montanus 56
  D. pusillus 25, 55, 56, 137, *137*
digestive tract 85
diseases and disorders 22–3
  bacterial 113–15
  fungal 112–13
  non-infectious 118–19
  parasites 115–18
  swim bladder disorders 118
Dowe's minnow 38–9
dropsy 118
Drosophila 91
dwarf livebearer 131, *131*
dwarf top-minnow 131, *131*

Echinodorus major 74, 82
  E. tenellus 74, *74*
eel grass 82
elfin goodeid 28, *28*
endangered species 18–19
exophthalmia *114*
eyes 58–9, *114*

feeding 84–91
  see also food
feeding ring 85
fertility 10
filtration systems 68–70
  power 69–70
  undergravel 68–9
fins 61, 62–3, 64–5, *65*,
Flexipenis 42–3
  F. vittatus 42, *42*
Floridichys carpio 83
food:
  color foods 86–7
  freeze dried 89
  frozen 89
  greenstuff 86
  live 87–91

meat 91
  storage 86
  terrestrial 90–1
  varying 91
  for young fish 105–6
four-eyed fish *38*, 58–9, 83, 123, *123*
fresh water, as habitat 11–12
fruit flies 91
fungal diseases 112–13

Gambusia 42, 43
  G. affinis 12, *12*, 17, 18
  G. amistadensis 19, 43
  G. gaigei 18–19, *18*
  G. holbrooki 12, 17, *17*, 132, *132*
  G. puncticulata 43
  G. speciosa 19
gender determination 99–100
genetics 107–9
German swordtails 109
gill flukes 116–17
Girardinichthys 33
  G. viviparus 33, *33*
Girardinus 9, 43–4
  G. metallicus 28, *29*, 43, *44*
gnat larva 88
gold-spotted killifish 83
golden bumblebee goodeid 30
golden sailfin goodeid *35*
golden teddy 53, *53*
gonopodium 62–4, 92, 98
Goodea 33–4
  G. atripinnis 33, 122, *122*
Goodeidae family 10, 29–37, 62, 63, 94, 120–2
gravid spot 99
green cobra guppy *49*

green goodeid *37*
green swordtail *54*
Greenway's livebearer 52, *52*
grindalworms 90
growth rates 106–7
guppies 13, *13*, 14–17, 39, 48–9, 62, 65, 67, 86, 93, 98, *99*, 101, 108, 110, 124–25, *124–25*
Guppy, John 6
Gyrodactylus 16–17, 117

halfbeaks 7, 8, 9, 55–7, 58, 84
hearing 60
Hemirhamphidae family 7, 8, 9, 55–7, 58, 137
Hemirhamphodon 56–7
  H. pogonognathus 56, 82, *82*
  H. tengah 56
Heterandria 44–5, 93, 94, 95, *99*
  H. formosa 44, 101, 131, *131*
Heterophallus 45
  H. rachowi 45
hormones, use of 63
hornwort 36, 82
Hottonia inflata 75
housing unsuitable companions 58
Hubbsina 34
  H. turneri 34
humpbacked limia 133, *133*
hybridization 95–7
Hyporhamphus 57

ich 23, 115–16
Ilyodon 34–5
  I. furcidens 34
  I. xantusi 34, *34*

Java fern 78–9, 82

Java moss 78, 82
Jenynsia 38, 94
  J. lineata 38
Jordanella floridae 83, 83

knife fish (knife livebearer)
  39–40, 70, 136, 136

large mosquito fish 132,
  132
lateral line 59–60
Latimeria chalumnae 8
'leap fish' 106
liberty molly 96
Limia 45, 48, 95
  L. caymenensis 45
  L. melonogaster 134, 134
  L. nigrofasciata 133, 133
  L. tridens 45
  L. vittata 119
livebearers
  adaptability 12
  buying 20–5
  distribution of 9–12
  evolution of 8
  foreign introduction 17
  habitat 12–13
  lifespan 110
  size 13
  survival advantages 10
long-snout halfbeak 56
lyretail 110

marigold needle swordtail
  129, 129
mating 62–4, 98–9
Melanotaenia 83
melanoma 119
merry widow 27, 46–7
metallic top minnow 28,
  29, 44
Mexican livebearers 29–37
Mexican oak-leaf plant 74,
  75
Micropoecilia 48, 49

M. picta 49
Microsorium pteropus
  78–9, 82
microworms 90, 106
mollies 23, 108
mono 83
Monodactylus argenteus
  83
Montezuma swordtail 55
moonfish 130, 130
mosquito fish 44, 93, 94,
  95, 98, 99, 101, 131,
  131
mosquito fish, eastern 17,
  132, 132
mosquito fish, western 17,
  18
mouth fungus 113
mouthparts 84

nauplii 89–90, 106
Neoheterandria 46
  N. elegans 46
Nomorhamphus 57
Nymphaea maculata 76

occasional live birth 93
orange-dorsal livebearer 27
orange-tailed goodeid 22
ovarian gestation 94
ovoviviparous species 93
Oxyzygonectes 38–9
  O. dowi/dovii 38–9

Pamphorichthys 50
parasites 16–17
Phallichthys 46–7
  P. amates amates 27,
    46–7, 46
  P. amates pittieri 27
Phalloceros 47
  P. caudimaculatus 47, 47
Phalloptychus 48
  P. eigenmanni 48
  P. januarius 48

Phallotorynus 48
pike cichlids 15, 16
pike livebearer/
  pike minnow 40, 40,
    62, 74, 85, 91, 135,
    135
piscine tuberculosis 114
platies 55, 55, 99, 100, 108,
  109, 119, 130, 130
Poecilia 48–50, 95
  P. formosa 94, 95, 96,
    100
  P. reticulata 13, 13, 14,
    16, 17, 62, 48–9, 49,
    65, 74, 86, 93, 99, 101,
    108, 110, 124, 125,
    124–5
  P. (Lebistes) reticulata 49
  P. latipinna 50, 61, 61,
    97, 107, 110, 127, 127
  P. lucida 100
  P. mexicana 96, 97
  P. (Molliensia)
    latipunctata 114
  P. sphenops 96, 73, 126,
    126
  P. sulphuraria 12
  P. variatus 108, 109
  P. velifera 114
Poeciliidae family 10, 18,
  39–55, 24–36
Poeciliinae 8–9
Poeciliopsis 50
  P. paucimaculata 50
porthole molly 114
predators 14–16
Priapella 50–1
  P. bonita 50
  P. intermedia 51
Priapichthys 51
  P. annectens 51
  P. a. hesperis 51
Pterophyllum 58
pygmy chain sword plant
  74, 74

quarantine 111
Quintana 51–2
  Q. atrizona 51–2, *51*

rainbow goodeid *32*, 121, *121*
red tuxedo swordtail 128, *128*
red wagtail swordtail *54*
red-tailed goodeid *36*
regal goodeid *30*
reproductive triggers 98, 101
respiration 61
Rivulus harti 14, *14*

sailfin molly 61, 97, *114*, 127, *127*
salinity levels 82
saltwater, as habitat 11
Saprolegnia 112
sawfin goodeids 35
scat 83
Scatophagus argus 83
Scolichthys 52
  S. greenwayi 52, *52*
sensory organs 58–60
sexing 23, 58, 107
Shinnersia rivularis *74*, 75
Siamese fighting fish 58
Skiffia 35
  S. bilineata 28, *28*
  S. francesae 35
skin flukes 117
small spot topminnow *50*
snails 75, 76
snakeskin triangletail *125*
spawning boxes 102–3
species, definition 26–8

sperm storage 93, 95
superfetation 95
swim bladder 60, 118
swordtails 23, *24*, *62*, 63 *86*, 98, 99, 101, 108, 128–9, *128-9*
  lyretailed 63, 64
  veiltail 64

tank, preparing 25
taxonomy 25–8
temperature 70–2, 83, 110
threadjaw halfbeak 82, *82*
Tiburon limia *45*
tiger barbs 58
Tomeurus 53
  T. gracilis 53
Tondanichthys 57
toothcarp 15
transporting 23–4
treatment tanks 111
triangletail 'nigrocaudatus' *124*
Trinidad 6, 9, 14
trophotaeniae 94
tropical water violet 75
tubifex worms 88, 89
two-lined skiffia 28, *28*

Vallisneria spiralis 82
velvet disease 116
Vesicularia dubyana 78, 82
viviparous species 93

water composition 79–83, 119
  additives 81
  conditioning 79, 81
  hardness 79, 80

pH levels 79–80
  testing 80–1, 119
white spot 115–16
whiteworms 90, *91*
Wiesbaden swordtails *109*
worms (food) 88–9, 90–1
worms (parasites) 117–18
wrestling halfbeak 25, 55, 137, *137*

Xantus' ilyodon *34*
Xenodexia 53
  X. ctenolepis 53
Xenophallus 53–4
  X. umbratilis 53, *53*
Xenophorus captivus 36
Xenotaenia 36
  X. resolanae 36
Xenotoca 36–7
  X. eiseni 22, *37*
Xiphophorus 54–5, 95, 119
  X. birchmanni 55
  X. cortezi 55
  X. helleri 10, 23, *24*, 54, *54*, *62*, 63, *66*, 68, 73, 87, *98*, *99*, 100, *101*, 102, 128–9
  X. maculatus 55, *55*, 68, 107, 108, 119, 130, *130*
  X. montezumae montezumae 55
  X. variatus *106*, 107, *112*, 128

Zenarchopterus 57
  Z. beauforti 57
Zoogoneticus 37
  Z. quitzeoensis 37, *37*
  Z. tequila 37